A
MODERN
MAN

A MODERN MAN

THE BEST OF
GEORGE CARLIN

FOREWORD BY
LEWIS BLACK

INTRODUCTION BY
JERRY HAMZA

 hachette
BOOKS   NEW YORK

Hachette Books
Hachette Book Group
1290 Avenue of the Americas
New York, NY 10104
HachetteBooks.com
Twitter.com/HachetteBooks
Instagram.com/HachetteBooks

First Anthology Edition: November 2021

Published by Hachette Books, an imprint of Perseus Books, LLC, a subsidiary of
Hachette Book Group, Inc. The Hachette Books name and logo is a trademark
of the Hachette Book Group.

The Hachette Speakers Bureau provides a wide range of authors for speaking events.
To find out more, go to www.hachettespeakersbureau.com or call (866) 376-6591.
The publisher is not responsible for websites (or their content) that are not owned
by the publisher.

Print book interior design by Jeff Williams

Library of Congress Control Number: 2021943934
ISBNs: 978-0-306-82709-9 (paperback), 978-0-306-82710-5 (ebook)

Printed in the United States of America

LSC-C

Printing 2, 2022

CONTENTS

FOREWORD

George Carlin.

If you do not know who he is, close this book now and buy it. I'm not telling you this to make money for George. Sadly he has passed on. I'm not telling you this to make money for me. I won't make a dime off a sale. I'm telling You this for You because You need to go home now and sit down and read this book from cover to cover.

WHY?

It will change your life, that is why.

REALLY?

Yes it will. Even if it totally offends You, which it just might. And how will that help You? You will be forced to understand and defend what you believe in that makes what George wrote so offensive to You. He will have made You think about your beliefs, and there is no greater gift one can give than to make another person actually think. Except for the other great gift he will give you if you are not offended, an even greater gift: You will laugh and You will think. Or You will think and You will laugh. And You will laugh really hard.

HOW DO I KNOW THAT?

Because he made me laugh so hard that when I stopped laughing I had changed. I saw the world in a different way. George made me realize something that I already knew but

didn't know how to express. That just because someone was
an authority figure didn't mean you had to trust them. It didn't
even mean they were much of an authority. He pointed out for
me all of the hypocrisy that was so much a part of the fabric
of the society I was a part of and yet felt separated from. His
voice made me feel that there was nothing wrong with that
feeling. He had fine-tuned my mind to be able to understand
and cope with the madness of the times I was living through.
Still, as you will find in this compendium of his writing as he
points out over and over, as much as things change the more
they stay the same.

And extraordinarily, even now, every day, every single day
someone somewhere will see something that will leave them
speechless and ask: "What would George Carlin have to say
about this?" After his death, he became more than just a man.
His name became synonymous with a change in consciousness. His words gave us, then and now, a new way to see the
world. He has been missed every day by countless folks everywhere looking for a really hard laugh at the darkest possible
moments.

HOW IS THAT POSSIBLE?

Because he was more than just a comic. He was a sage, a
philosopher, and a prophet—and most importantly, as you will
learn when you read this book, George was a writer, wonderful, profound, and funny, so fucking funny. There was nothing
fancy in his writing. It went straight to the gut.

With a spectacular wit, he showed how hypocritical our
lives had become and he did it by going after the hypocrisy
he saw in his own act. In front of our eyes he went through a
metamorphosis that reflected the culture he was living in, that
we were living in, that I was living in. He went from being a
comic who was a part of the establishment to one who was

anti-establishment. To put it more simplistically, we watched his hair go from short to long.

But it was more than being representative of the changing times: he sensed we could be better than we were. He didn't use dirty words (idiotic to call any words dirty, as he and others before pointed out) to shock us but to teach us. By *us*, I mean all generations, young to old, from me to my dad. Parents and their kids together would watch the early, mainstream George Carlin in his numerous TV appearances. Later on, parents might wait till the kids were asleep to listen to those first groundbreaking albums of his and the kids might grab them and listen to them in the basement. They'd both listen and keep George a secret. The parents didn't want their kids to find the album and listen to him, and the kids didn't want their parents to know they were listening to him. And that's how you know he was special.

My father (who had seen Nichols and May, Lenny Bruce, and other comedy legends perform live) was a huge fan of George Carlin. To give you an understanding of just how big a fan he was, when I was nominated for an American Comedy Award in 2000 for Male Stand-Up Comic, I asked my parents if they wanted to go to the awards ceremony with me. My father said no. It was in Los Angeles, so I thought maybe he wasn't up for a long flight. Then I told him that George was being given a Lifetime Achievement Award that night. My father said, "That's well deserved. If I went, do you think I could maybe meet him?" I said, "I think so." My father said, "Okay, then, I'll go." All of a sudden it wasn't that long a flight. My father loved me, but he'd fly out there to meet George. I approached George that night to see if he could take a moment to meet my dad and he graciously said yes. He was generous with his time. My father got to meet George Carlin. It took a few days for him to stop smiling and it wasn't because I won the award. I wasn't jealous.

There are a few comics whose writing is as strong as their performance is. George's performances were brilliant as he was a wonderful physical comic, but his writing was magical. He chose his words meticulously, not only for the sound but for the precision of their meaning. George had a deep love of music and his acts were scored like they were music. Words were his notes.

I could tell you about all of my favorite George Carlin comedy routines. But if you know him, you already have your own and your reasons why they are. If you don't, you will discover them within these pages, and I guarantee if you listen to just one of his albums you will hear his voice when you read his words.

Much of what you are about to read is as profound as it is historic. That may seem like an overstatement. It is not.

To have an idea of the effect his albums had on countless listeners, imagine sitting in your basement and dropping the needle onto the vinyl. It is much, I believe, how it must have been as if you were in the presence of the primitive man who showed up at your cave for the first time with fire.

But in the end,

There is only one reason to buy this book,

It is seriously funny.

You won't regret it.

And you will laugh.

Really really hard.

—*Lewis Black*

INTRODUCTION

I first met George Carlin in March 1976.

At that time, I was working for my father as a promoter. I had a hard time working for him—he was tough to work for. So I went out on my own and accumulated some properties to make some rental income. Meanwhile, he still wanted me to get on the road and get killed out there, driving from show to show, working for three hundred bucks a week. I used to be jealous of the people inside watching *Gunsmoke*. I'd see smoke coming out of their chimneys, and I'd be out in the snow following trailer trucks. I finally quit. I said, "You know, you're terrific to work for," which was one of the bigger lies in my life, and I told him, "I can't do this anymore. I don't like the driving; I don't like being away from home. My heart's not in it."

My father and mother were divorced, but they were still close. He started going to my mother every day: "What's he going to be, a bum?" he'd ask her. But I was very happy to sleep 'til one o'clock and collect my rent. And then one day my father came to me. "Listen," he said. "I've got something for ya. You don't have to travel, we can play Rochester and Syracuse, and it's not country music. It's not the same thing you've been doing for all these years, and his name is George Carlin." I did not even know who he was.

My father told me a friend of his booked George in Toledo, and they sold out 2,500 seats. But he didn't show up. He was loaded. "Oh, that's fucking great," I said. Still, my father wanted to give it a shot. So we tried Rochester and Syracuse and sold out both dates.

The day of the show, I had an interview request from the *Syracuse Herald-Journal*. Now, you don't make a request for that on such short notice, but the paper did, and I said I'd ask him. George walked into his dressing room and closed the door. I said, "Hi, I'm Jerry. We got a request from the paper to do an interview." And the first thing he ever said to me was, "Why? Is it my birthday?" So, he never did that interview.

After the first shows, I started to learn how hooked he still was on coke. George used to drink twenty beers a day, smoking pot all the time, doing coke all the time. He would be out onstage, and he'd be doing great, then he'd forget what he was doing for maybe twenty seconds, which might not sound like much, but for the stage that's quite a while. Then it'd come back to him, and he'd go back to his act. He was a mess.

But he *was* funny. After those two sellout dates in March, I got George five more dates in May. One of them, the sixth Carlin show I ever presented, was in Hartford, Connecticut, at the prestigious Bushnell Hall. The manager there was Leverett Wright. He wore a blue pinstripe suit, had gray hair, and was a very commanding sort of person, very formal. He managed Mantovani, who led a big orchestra from England. Anyway, he called me up to his office—he'd heard about George Carlin's material and asked me to remind George that Bushnell Hall was dedicated to our war dead. Well, I told George, and then George went out and did the filthiest show I ever heard him do. I learned early that he hated authority with a passion.

So that's how we got started. We got friendly. He never said much; he was usually coked up. He had a roadie who would always have five lines of coke in his dressing room in front of the mirror at intermission or in between shows if we had two shows.

That wasn't his only problem. George was trying to do a movie with his wife, and that really broke him financially. He didn't pay his taxes for three years. He had people on payroll who were running around like Jack Warner, and they never shot one piece of film. His wife met a guy in AA, and he was going to be the director/producer, even though he had never done anything. And then he had his daughter's horse farm to support.

It was a disastrous time, but he wasn't down. He still had enough to sell out two-thousand-seat theaters. And I could look at him and say, "You know, I know he screwed up, but he's really smart."

He had two managers at this point—his old manager plus the guy producing the movie—and he wanted a new one. I was miserable myself with my father, so I said, "Why don't you give me a chance?" He did give me a chance, and it's a good thing he did. Together, we were probably as successful as any team in the history of the business, like Ella Fitzgerald and Norman Granz.

• • •

George had a saying: "I didn't lick it off the rocks." He meant that what talent he had, he got from his parents and his family.

His father was a violent drunk who couldn't metabolize alcohol. He would take George's older brother Patrick into a bar and kid around with him, and if he didn't like the answers, he'd slap him around. He had a violent side, and he really messed Patrick up. But he was a very brilliant man. As a matter of fact, he entered the Andrew Carnegie speaking contest in New York. I guess there were about two thousand people, and he won it. So, you know he was on the ball.

George's mother was determined that none of this was going to happen to George, so she left her husband. George never knew his father and told me in the car many times that he was glad. George was a sensitive guy. He wasn't tough at all. He could talk that way, but that was all a front. And if he had to live with a father who was going to slap the shit out of him, it would have broken him. And he knew it, so he was glad he never knew his father.

Even though George always had problems with his mother, she loved her boys, especially George—he was her baby. She was a husbandless mother with two young boys in the late 1930s, and she did everything to raise them right. She was a head secretary to a big shot at a newspaper and she had to struggle for money. When George was ten years old, she bought him a tape recorder—it's funny, I had one, too—and he used this to learn how to mimic his favorite comics and actresses. He got good at it! He was a little boy, and he'd be doing W. C. Fields or whomever and, you know, I think that was a good investment.

He always had that talent. In the eighth grade, he was kicked out of school. And the nuns told him they wouldn't let him back in unless he wrote a play. Years later, he'd have nuns from his grammar school show up at his concerts, filthy language and all. He'd have the nuns onstage after the show, and they loved him.

· · ·

In the early 1970s, George had four hit albums that went through the roof. All four went gold, and *FM & AM* won a

Grammy. And then things started going downhill. As you put out more albums, fewer and fewer people would buy them. George, at the same time, was terrifically loaded with cocaine, pot, LSD if he could get his hands on it. So he would be home lying in bed, couldn't do anything professionally. Meanwhile, his career diminished. The only way they remembered George Carlin was once or twice a year he would get to host Johnny Carson's show. That would get him some attention, but outside of that there was no attention, and it was just fading away. At the same time, Steve Martin exploded.

By the time I started working with him, he wasn't red-hot anymore, but he still had a little heat from the albums. Early on, George had a contract with the Sahara hotel to do two shows a night, and it was for a lot of money. And the reason he had that show is because he made it when he was hot, with those first four albums. Now, he couldn't draw flies. These shows were drawing like three hundred people, and so they came to me and asked, could we get rid of some shows? "Can we knock it down to one show?" And I felt like a prick but I said to myself, "Shit, we need the money desperately here. We're not doing anything." So I held on and we got the money and we started to move.

It wasn't easy at first. Before I had HBO ready to go, I figured I would start with interviews to get him attention. I set him up with magazines that would give him good articles; the problem was that all they wanted to talk about was George and his struggle with drugs. Nobody wanted to talk about comedy, it was all drugs. And George didn't like it. One time, his wife was visiting her family in Dayton, Ohio, and George got pissed off at all of these drug interviews he was doing in New York, and he got pretty well drunk and drove to Dayton to meet his wife and smashed into a telephone pole and broke his nose.

HBO is what really brought him back, though. There was a guy named Michael Fuchs that ran HBO in the beginning. Fuchs loved George and he wanted George in the worst way because of the language. He would advertise, *You could hear anything you want on my network*. And plus, George was funny.

So I got him in there to do that show for HBO, and after that we did thirteen more in a row. He was the most successful comedian in the history of HBO. That's what kept him going—every two years we would do a show for HBO. After every show he'd say, "This is the last one." And then three weeks later he'd say, "You know, Jerry, I was adding up the material. We've got thirty-eight minutes! All we got to do is add twenty minutes and we could do another show." At that time, an album or something—that era was over. It was television that was gonna fuel his career.

That was never enough, though—he still had to tour. He loved getting in front of a crowd, but he absolutely hated going on the road. When he heard Willie Nelson's "On the Road Again," he thought Willie was nuts. He did not understand that some people could actually enjoy it, because he hated packing his bag and leaving his home. He wanted to quit the road and he wanted to be home writing. It never happened; he had to go on the road and pay his bills.

Now, he needed the show; it was like a tonic for him, to go out and do a concert for people. That helped him, but every other part of it, he hated. He especially hated meet-and-greets. In my business, if you do a promotion for a record company, you've got to meet the boss; do something for an Indian casino, they like to have you meet the chief after the show. George hated it, but he did it every single time, and he was absolutely perfect at it. He was just so warm and professional and nice to these people. And afterward he'd say, "Well, that was all right, but try not to make me do that again."

He hated the road. The packing, the planning, the airplanes. He just couldn't handle it. You know, Willie Nelson was in a million-dollar bus watching TV or something, and we were in a rental car driving around. George wanted to be home writing.

George was a stand-up, but he considered himself a writer. When he could, he'd hang around at home, smoking joints and listening to bebop and writing. He always had to have company when he wrote, on the radio or with a record. Somebody had to be singing, somebody had to be talking. Baseball, a basketball game, something had to be going on in the background; he could never just sit there and write. I guess he was too neurotic.

We spent a lot of time on the road together. I was on the road with him for thirty-five years. Eventually, we became best friends. And the nicest part, creatively, was, if a guy gets off a stage and in a car at twelve o'clock and we go to a gas station and get some pretzels and some cokes and maybe some beer, by the time he comes down, he's loose. It's different. He's not uptight anymore. And we would throw these ideas around. And if I threw a good one at him, he would write it down, and two months later it would be a ten-minute piece for HBO.

George was a disc jockey before he was a stand-up. He became very friendly with this guy that owned a radio station—it was a Southern station. And George told me the guy that owned it gave him the best advice he probably ever had in his life. He said, "Whenever you get a funny thought, whatever you're thinking about—write it down!" And George took that to heart and wrote everything down. And this way he always had all this material coming out of him like mad.

He wasn't always easy to be around, but we never fought. He was always impatient, and he was irritably depressed. I would fly with him from Los Angeles to New York, and he might not say two words other than "Here, I've gotta hit the john." Not what people would expect. People would ask me— how was it working for him throughout the years? It must have been a blast. But the truth is that it was very quiet, and the best material we came up with was in a rental car after the show, when he was coming down, at two or three in the morning. But during the day there wasn't much he would say, and he was the way he was. He wasn't happy to be out on the road, and he wasn't happy in general.

He hated to queue up for anything. In the beginning, up until 9/11, we always flew commercial. And George would try to be first in line to get on an airplane so that he could get the overhead space. Sometimes somebody would beat him to it, and he would get pretty angry, which was stupid—I mean it was illogical. He would say: "Mr. CEO, you would grab that spot right over my seat. Mr. CEO . . ." I'm much bigger than him, and I remember saying he's not going to get himself killed, he's going to get me killed!

He canceled a concert in Corpus Christi, Texas, twice because he had in his mind that terrorists were going to blow up the oil fields down there. Can you believe it? He canceled it twice, and I had to go to the guy who managed the theater and say he's having problems, he's not feeling well. The truth of it was that he was neurotic about these terrorists. After 9/11, we started flying private. There was no way he was gonna fly commercial after that.

The drugs didn't help. He always loved cocaine. He called it *girl*, maybe that's what everybody called it—I don't know, maybe because it was seductive. He told me he quit, but I'm not sure that he ever quit because he kept that away from me. He would tell people, his friends in New York, if they decided to do something: "Don't tell Jerry." Ain't that funny? Like I was his father, or something.

One day, George's wife told him that I was like a father to him. And he said, "No, a brother." He was right. I wasn't just his manager or his best friend; we were brothers.

He looked at things differently than other people. He was a brilliant man. One day we were having a Thanksgiving over at this house, and they had a ham over there. And he had a black dog that jumped up and grabbed the rest of the ham. The dog had the ham in his mouth and ran out the house. And when I saw George, he told me, "If you see a dog shaped like a ham running down your street, call me. It's my dog." Nobody would think like that. He just had that.

What happened to George—he started out talking about dogs and cats but what really made him is that he got philosophical. He started coming up with ideas about life on our planet and are we gonna make it. Crooked politicians. He predicted a virus coming to kill us. He didn't have much hope for the planet. He thought we were fucked. He was pretty public about this, and people related to it. George used to say there's a club of the people who make all the money, and guess what? We're not in it. I hear that so much from people. They feel it, and they believe it, and I believe it. I mean, Christ, there's people that are multibillionaires and there's people who don't know where their next ham sandwich is coming from. So, they related to him, and they understood him.

I had a deal for him once with Fuji Photo. We needed the money to pay his taxes, and he booked a commercial for Fuji Photo and they gave him a million bucks and we immediately turned it over to the government. George hated doing this. He thought he betrayed himself by doing that commercial. He thought he never should've done it. But he couldn't tell me. He knew how hard I was struggling to come up with the money to keep this circus going. Well, Fuji Photo has an office somewhere near Newark, New Jersey, and we did a show there. He went out onstage in front of all these big shots from Fuji, very conservative Japanese businesspeople. And he went out and started talking about Ronald Reagan and his criminal gang, and that was the end of it. We never heard anything more from Fuji Photo. I said, "You son of a bitch, why didn't you just tell me you weren't . . ." That's how he was. He cared enough about me that he didn't want to come and tell me, "I ain't doing it." At the same time, he had his principles.

George never forgot where he came from. He was working-class all the way, Dodgers over the Yankees. He'd always go for the underdogs. He was never arrogant about who he was. He was always especially kind to working people because that's where he came from. Once, George and I heard Sinatra on the radio call people "little people," and George said, "Fuck that prick. There are no little people." So he definitely considered himself part of the working class, no matter how much he had, no matter how famous he became. He was always with those guys. He grew up with them, and he stayed with them. If you hit him the wrong way, boy, he had a silver tongue that could cut you up. Like he was in a fencing contest. But he knew who he was, and he was never arrogant.

One of the things that made George so popular was that he would come up with a thought—it would be a *brainy* thought— he'd write it into a routine, and people would hear it and say, "Hey, that's the way I think!" So they related to him like he was one of their own. And he really was. George hated when other comedians would talk about money. He felt that that had no place in a comic's life. And I agree with him. People don't listen to comedians to hear that they're worth $100 million. In all the years I was with him, I saw him get angry, I saw this and that, but I never saw him get snooty or snobbish or look down on anybody.

It's important to know that despite the fame, George spoke often of his grammar school friends. He loved the kids that he grew up with and he told me that they were the best people he met in his life, the kids that he met before he got kicked out of the eighth grade. He just loved them and would invite them to concert after concert. And if his friends were anywhere near New York City, and George was doing a concert, they would show up.

He invited a lot of his friends to see Carlin at Carnegie, which was something that I pushed for on HBO . . . I just loved the alliteration. And we had to come back; we were doing no business. Steve Martin was out there doing ten thousand to fifteen thousand people, and we were doing five hundred to eight hundred people, couldn't even pay the transportation or opening act. And when he did Carlin at Carnegie, that's really what brought him back.

The setup for the show wasn't perfect. We were put into a situation where we needed a date. I had to grab a date, 'cause we needed it. We couldn't do a safety show the night before. When we got done with that show, we went down to the basement at Carnegie Hall and he actually had tears come out of his eyes because he felt that he could've done better.

Since his death, people asked me if I miss him (duh). Some will ask what I miss most about him, and I will say (after giving it a good think) that I lost my teacher. I learned much about comedy and language from George. But there was so much more. George loved science and kept up with it and passed it to me. I also learned it was definitely pronounced "Keltics," not "Seltics." When you read this book you will get a very funny infusion of his teaching, a taste of what I got over thirty-five years traveling, working, and shooting the shit with my best friend.

Have fun.

—*Jerry Hamza*

A
MODERN
MAN

THE PRIMITIVE SERGEANT

There was a first time for everything. At some point, every custom, every practice, every ritual had to be explained to people for the first time. It must have been tricky, especially in primitive societies.

For instance, the first human sacrifice. Not of the enemy, but the first ritual killing of a member of your own tribe. Someone had to announce it to the people. Someone with authority, but probably not the top guy. A sergeant. A primitive sergeant, addressing a band of early cave people—hunters, gatherers, whatever—explaining the human sacrifice. Of course, first he would have to get his other announcements out of the way.

"OK, listen up! You people in the trees, you wanna pay attention? The guys in the bushes, would ya put the woman down? All right. Now, is everybody here? Andy, check the caves. Make sure everybody's out here. And Andy, . . . don't wake up the bears! OK? Remember what happened last time. We can't spare any more people.

"OK, a few things I wanna go over, then I'm gonna tell ya about somethin' new. Somethin' we haven't tried before, so I don't want ya to be nervous. I know ya don't like new things. I remember last year a lotta people freaked out when someone came up with the wheel. People went nuts! They said, Well, this is it, it's all over, it's the end of the world, bla, bla, bla.

Then somebody pointed out that we didn't have any axles. I think it was Richie. He said if we really wanted to invent something special, we oughta come up with the axle. I guess you're always gonna have a coupla wise guys.

"But anyway, we went ahead and made a coupla hundred of these big stone wheels, which is kinda stupid when you think about it. The only thing you can do with 'em is roll 'em down the hill. Which isn't such a top notch idea. I think the people who live at the bottom of the hill will bear me out on that.

"OK, movin' along here. It has come to my attention that some people have been drawin' pictures on the walls of the caves. Pictures of bulls, antelopes, a coupla horses. I think I even seen a goat on one wall. Listen, lemme tell you somethin'. It might seem like fun to you, but it looks awful. If ya can't keep the place clean, maybe ya don't deserve a nice cave. Ya don't see the bats drawin' pictures on the walls, do ya? No. They hang upside down, they take a crap, they don't bother anybody.

"You people don't know when you're well off. Maybe ya'd like to go back to livin' in the trees, huh? Remember that? Remember the trees? Competin' with the baboons and gibbons for hazelnuts and loganberries? Degrading! So there'll be no more drawin' on the walls! Coupla thousand years from now, people are gonna come here, and they're gonna study these caves. The last thing they wanna see is a lotta horse pictures on the walls.

"OK, continuin' on. As some of you mighta noticed, last night the fire went out. Coupla the guys on guard duty were jackin' around, playin' grabass, and one of 'em, Octavio, the short guy with the bushy hair. Well, one of the short guys with the bushy hair. Anyways, Octavio fell on the fire, and the fire went out. Unfortunately for Octavio, he died in the incident. Unfortunately for us, he was the only one who knew how to light the fire. So we're gonna have a contest. The first guy to get a fire goin', and keep it goin', wins a prize. It's a hat. Nothin' fancy. Just a regular hat. The kind with the earlaps.

"OK, next item. We're startin' to get some complaints from the women about dating procedures. This mainly concerns the practice of clubbin' the women on the head and draggin' 'em back to the cave by the hair. They would like to discontinue this practice, especially the hair part. It seems some of them go to a lot of trouble and expense to fix up their hair for a date, and they feel the draggin' has a negative effect on their appearance. As far as the clubbin' is concerned, they'd like to elminate that too, because what happens is a lot of 'em have an enjoyable date, and then they can't remember it in the mornin'.

"Movin' right along. As you all know, it's been our practice when we find a new plant that looks good to eat, we test it on the dogs to see if it's poison. Does everyone remember the berries we tested last week on the big brown dog? How many ate the berries simply because the dog didn't die that day? Quite a few. Well, I got bad news. The dog died last night. Apparently it was a slow-actin' poison. Yes, Laszlo? You didn't eat the berries? But this mornin' you ate the dog. Well, Laszlo, ya got about a week. Food chain! How many times do I gotta tell you people? Food chain! By the way, anyone who's gettin' into that new cannibalism crap—I won't mention any names—I'd strongly suggest not eatin' Laszlo—or anyone else for that matter.

"All right, now we gotta talk about the Hated Band of Enemy People Who Live in the Dark Valley. As some of ya might know, they snuck into camp last night and stole a bunch of our stuff. They got those sticks we were savin'. They got the rocks we piled up near the big tree. And they also took sixteen trinkets; the ones we got in a trade with the Friendly Bent-over People from the Tall Mountain Near the Sun. I think it was them. It was either them or the Guys with the Really Big Foreheads Down by the River. Anyways, as I recall, we came off a cool two hundred animal skins for those trinkets, and frankly, the Chief and I think we got screwed. By the way, speakin' of screwin', they also stole several of our women last night. Along with a couple of those sensitive men we've been usin' as women.

"OK, a new problem has come up that we're gonna have to deal with. It concerns the growin' menace of people chewin' the leaves of the dream plant. It's gotten completely outta hand. At first it wasn't so bad. After a long day of huntin', or gatherin'—whatever—people would chew a coupla leaves to relax. Recreational chewin'. No harm, no foul. But then some guys couldn't leave it alone. They would chew way too much and lose control. Some of them became verbally abusive. Of course, they couldn't help what they were sayin.' It wasn't them talkin', it was the leaves. But, hey, nevertheless!

"Then we found out some people were chewin' on the job. Not only endangerin' the lives of their co-hunters or co-gatherers—whatever—but also lowerin' the amount of food we acquire, while somehow, at the same time, greatly increasin' the rate of consumption of their own food. One of the gatherers, a short guy with bushy hair, I think it was Norris, got whacked outta his skull on leaves last week, and he came in from gatherin', with a grand total . . . get this . . . a grand total of six berries and one nut. And this guy had been out in the bushes for eight days!

"But now we're runnin' into an even more serious problem that affects the safety of everyone. It seems that some people are chewin' the leaves and then runnin' around in circles at high speed. As a result we're startin' to get a huge increase in the number of accidents. People are crashin' into each other. Please! Try to remember. Chewin' and runnin' around in circles at high speed don't mix. If you're gonna run around in circles, don't chew; and if you're gonna chew, for God's sake, don't be runnin' around in circles. Designate someone.

"So try to be aware of the signs of leaf abuse. If you're chewin' in the mornin', you got a problem. If you're chewin' alone, you got a problem. It's no disgrace. Get some help. Say no to leaves.

"OK, now, like I said earlier, we got a new thing we're gonna be doin', and I wanna announce it today. It's gonna be a custom. Remember customs? Who can name a custom? Nat? Goin' to sleep at night? Well, that's close, Nat. That's almost like a custom. Who else can name a custom? Killing the animals before we eat them? OK, actually, Jules, that's more like a necessity, isn't it? More like a necessity. Lookin' for a custom. Another custom. Dwayne? Washin' the rocks and dryin' them off before you throw them at the enemy durin' a rock fight? Is that what you been doin', Dwayne? Really! Well, I guess that would explain the disproportionately high number of rock injuries in your squad, wouldn't it?

"Anyway, this new custom is quite different, and it might come as somethin' of a surprise to ya, so make sure you're sittin' down. Or at least leanin' on somethin' firm. You people standin' over near the cliff, you might wanna drift over this way a little.

"Now. I want ya to remember that no matter what I say, this is gonna please the Corn God. OK? [Slowly, as if to children] The new custom . . . is gonna help . . . with the corn. Remember a coupla years ago we had no corn, and we hadda eat the trees? And a lotta people died? How many wanna go back to eatin' the trees? OK, I rest my case. Yeah? Dwayne? You thought the trees were pretty good? Ya never disappoint me, Dwayne, ya know that? Folks, ya don't have to look very far for a tragic example of abusin' the dream plant, do ya?

"All right, here's the new thing we're gonna do, it's called a human sacrifice. Each week, to appease the Corn God, we're gonna kill one member of the tribe. All right, calm down! C'mon, sit down! Hey! Hold on! Hear me out on this, would ya? Just relax and hear me out on this. We're gonna start havin' a human sacrifice every week, probably on Saturday night. That's when everybody seems to loosen up pretty good. So startin' next Saturday night, about the time we run outta berry juice, we're gonna pick one person, probably a young virgin, and we'll throw her in the volcano. All right, girls! Please! Siddown! Please! Stop with the rocks!! Calm down, ladies. We're not gonna do it today. I promise. Relax.

"OK, so we throw the virgin in the volcano. By the way, how many remember the volcano? Remember the fire? Remember the lava? What word comes to mind when we think about the volcano? Hot! Right. The volcano is hot. What's that, Dwayne? No. No way. If this idea's gonna work at all, it's gotta be done while the volcano is actually erupting. I don't think the Corn God is gonna be impressed if we throw some chick in a dormant volcano. It's meaningless. I think he's lookin' for somethin' with a little more screamin' involved.

"OK, so we throw the virgin in the volcano. What's that? How does this help with the corn? Good question. Look, Morley, I just make the announcements, OK? I'm not involved with policy. It came down from the high priests, that's all you gotta know. This is one of those things you just gotta accept on faith. It's like that custom we started last year of cuttin' off a guy's head to keep him from stealin'. At first it seemed severe, am I right? But ya gotta admit, it seems to work.

"OK, one last point: You say, Why does it have to be a young virgin; why can't we throw a wrinkled old man in the volcano? Lemme put it this way. Did y'ever get a real good, close look at the high priests? OK. Once again, I rest my case.

"Now, the only problem we anticipate with this new custom is the distinct possibility of runnin' out of virgins. Ya gotta figure best case scenario we're not gonna see any corn till late next year, so it looks like we're gonna be waxin' virgins at quite a clip. And hey! . . . girls, don't take this the wrong way . . . but we don't have that many virgins to begin with, do we? Ha-ha-ha-ha!! No offense, girls! Really! No, hey, you're very lovely.

"Well, that's it, folks. Thanks for listenin'. Good night. Walk home slowly. And walk safely. In case you didn't notice, the sun went down, and it's completely fuckin' dark."

FUN FOES

Since I hold no real national allegiances, when it comes to armed conflict around the world I tend to root for the side that will provide me with the most entertainment. Saddam Hussein is a case in point. Any head of state who says, "We will walk on your corpses and crush your skulls, and you will swim in your own blood," is my kinda guy. You just don't hear that kind of shit anymore. This man obviously has great potential to provide me with amusing diversion.

In fact, all these Middle-East religious fanatics are brimming with entertainment potential. On CNN I recently saw video of 200 Islamic student–suicide bombers who were graduating from suicide-bomber school. They were singing what was apparently the school fight song: "Our blessings to you who fight at the gates of the enemy and knock on heaven's door with his skulls in your hands." How can Christians and Jews ever hope to compete with these folks who obviously enjoy their work so much?

LET'S ALL KILL EACH OTHER
ACCORDING TO THE RULES

I don't understand the Geneva Convention and the whole idea of having rules for fighting a war. Why? Is it really more than just a way of reassuring ourselves we're all quite civilized, as we pour our hearts and minds and fortunes into mass killing? It seems to me like hypocritical bullshit. If the object is to win, wars should be fought with no holds barred; otherwise, why bother suiting up? As it is now, a winner is declared, and yet the issue has not been settled by all possible means.

Additionally, if the object is to kill the enemy, why treat their wounded? Treating their wounded requires resources taken from your own effort to achieve victory. Does this make sense if you're trying to win? Oh, yeah. Civilized.

My doubts about having rules for combat likewise extend to street fighting. I've heard guys whine about someone throwing a "sucker punch." Are they kidding? A guy wants to reduce your ass to a small bloody pile, and you're going to warn him before hitting him? Get fucking lucid! And lose all that dopey shit about fair play. It's out of place if the object is to win. (Is it?)

Also, as far as kicking someone when he's down is concerned, what is the problem here? Again, the object is to win, yes? Well, if he gets up, you might lose; therefore he must not get up. He needs to be kicked. You said you wanted to win. Or are you people just fucking around? I suspect that might be the case. Well, stop fucking around and make up your mind. You're telling me a man will fuck another man's wife, drive him out of business, cut him off and nearly kill him in traffic, but he shouldn't sneak punch, or kick him when he's down? I don't get it.

Another thing I don't understand is the objection to so-called dirty play in sports such as football. These are big, tough guys who are desperate to prove how manly they are; that they're not soft. That's why they play these games in the first place. Well, why not let them play "dirty" and let's find out how tough they really are?

It's been shown that small, dedicated groups of men can easily find ways of policing and disciplining those among them who cross the line. It's called vigilantism, and it's very efficient. Please don't tell a bunch of six-foot-six, three hundred-pounders in helmets and pads they can't spear and punch and put their thumbs in each other's eyes. You'll miss all the fun. And you'll be keeping them from pursuing their calling at its highest level.

I also don't understand terrorists who call the police to warn them about a bomb. Do I need even explain my dismay at this one?

You know, folks, if this old world had any imagination, wars would be fought without codes and conventions, alley fighting would be standard, and the only rules in sports would govern the uniforms. Then we'd have some real fun.

But I fear that doesn't suit you, and so I return to the notion that produced these thoughts in the first place: You people shouldn't be fighting at all.

IF ONLY WE WERE HUMAN

This species is a dear, hateful, sweet, barbaric, tender, vile, intelligent, confused, virtuous, evil, thoughtful, perverted, generous, greedy species. In short, great entertainment.

As I said before, humans are the only species that systematically tortures and murders its own for pleasure and personal gain. In fact, we are the only species that systematically tortures and murders its own, period.

We are serial killers. All our poems and symphonies and oils on canvas will never change that. Man's noble aspect is the aberration.

Those who argue that art and philosophy are proof of human worth neglect to mention that, in the scheme we have devised, artists and philosophers are completely powerless and largely without prestige. Art, music, and philosophy are merely poignant examples of what we might have been had not the priests and traders gotten hold of us.

Most animals, when fighting one of their own, will show aggressive behavior, but very little hostility or intention to harm. And when the outcome of the struggle is inevitable, the losing animal will signal its defeat by exposing its most vulnerable part to the victor, affording it the opportunity to finish the kill. The victor then walks away without inflicting further harm. These are the creatures we feel superior to.

EUPHEMISMS:
IT'S A WHOLE NEW LANGUAGE

Euphemistic language turns up in many areas of American life in a variety of situations. Not all euphemisms are alike, but they have one thing in common: They obscure meaning rather than enhance it; they shade the truth. But they exist for various reasons.

Sometimes they simply replace a word that makes people uncomfortable. For instance, the terms *white meat*, *dark meat*, and *drumstick* came into use because in Victorian times people didn't like to mention certain body parts. No one at the dinner table really wanted to hear Uncle Herbert say, "Never mind the *thighs*, Margaret, let me have one of those nice, juicy *breasts*." It would've made them uncomfortable.

And at the same time, for the same reason, *belly* became *stomach*. But even *stomach* sounded too intimate, so they began saying *tummy*. It's actually a bit sad.

I first became aware of euphemisms when I was nine years old. I was in the living room with my mother and my aunt Lil when I mentioned that Lil had a *mole* on her face. My mother was quick to point out that Lil didn't have a mole, she had a *beauty mark*.

That confused me because, looking at Lil, the beauty mark didn't seem to be working. And it confused me further, because my uncle John also had a brown thing on his face, and it was clearly not a beauty mark. And so on that day, I discovered that on some people what appeared to be moles were actually beauty marks. And as it turned out, they were the same people whose *laugh lines* looked a lot like *crow's-feet*.

By the way, that whole beauty-mark scam worked so well that some women routinely began using eyebrow pencils to apply fake beauty marks—a "fake mole" being something no self-respecting woman would ever think of giving herself. Somehow, I can't imagine Elizabeth Taylor turning to Joan Crawford and saying, "Lend me your eyebrow pencil, Joanie, I'm gonna put a fake mole on my face."

By the way, it was only a few years after the Aunt Lil incident that I took comfort in the fact that some people apparently thought my ugly *pimples* were nothing more than minor *skin blemishes*.

Another role euphemisms play is to simply put a better face on things, to dress up existing phrases that sound too negative. *Nonprofit* became *not-for-profit*, because nonprofit sounded too much as though someone didn't know what they were doing. Not-for-profit makes it clear that there was never any intention of making a profit in the first place.

But some words that are euphemized aren't even vaguely negative, they're merely considered too ordinary. For that reason, many things that used to be *free* are now *complimentary*. Asking the hotel clerk if the newspapers are free makes you sound like a mooch, but "Are the newspapers complimentary?" allows you to retain some small bit of dignity. This is the reason some hotels offer their guests *complimentary continental breakfasts*, while others give their customers *free doughnuts*.

If you're one who would enjoy a closer look at euphemisms, you'll find a number of sections in the book that will interest you. I broke the euphemisms into segments, because they play such a large and varied role in American speech. And I call it The New Language, because it's certainly new to me; I know I didn't grow up with it. And that's my larger point: that it's gotten worse over time. There were probably a few early signs I noticed, but I knew the problem was getting serious when I began to hear ordinary people refer to *ideas* as *concepts*.

More to come.

PEACE ON YOU

I'm not disturbed by war. More like entertained. War may be a lot of things, but it's never a bad show. It's the original Greatest Show on Earth. Otherwise, why would they call it a "theater of war"? I love it. And as far as I'm concerned, the show must go on.

But I realize there are some people who really worry about this kind of thing, and so, as a good citizen, I offer two ideas for peace. It's the least I can do.

Many people work on war plans; not too many work on peace plans. They even have a war college at Ft. McNair, Washington. They call it the National Defense University, but it's a war college. They don't have a peace college.

And they have war plans for every contingency, no matter how remote. If Easter Island gives us some crap tomorrow, we have a plan in a computer that tells us exactly how to thoroughly bomb the shit out of Easter Island. You name the country, we've got the plan. Chad, Myanmar, Upper Volta, Burkina Faso, Liechtenstein. Just give us some crap, and we'll come there, and bomb the shit out of you! 'Cause we've got a plan.

Well, so do I. Two of them. George's plans for peace:

My first plan is worldwide, year-round, nonstop folk danc- ing. In short, everyone in the world would be required to dance all the time. It leaves very little time for fighting, and what combat does occur is inefficient, because the combatants are constantly in motion.

When it was suggested that this plan might be impractical, I offered an alternative wherein only half the people would be dancing at any given time. The problem with this was the distinct possibility that while half the people were dancing, the other half would be robbing their homes.

So now I've stripped it down to a symbolic plan: twenty-four-hour, nonstop, worldwide folk dancing, once a year. Each year, on a designated day, everyone in the world would stop what they were doing and dance for twenty-four hours.

Any kind of dancing you want. Square dance, minuet, grind, peabody, cakewalk, mazurka, samba, mashed potato. Doesn't matter. Just get out there and dance. Even hospital patients, shut-ins, cripples, and people on life support; if you're too sick to dance, you just die. While the doctors and nurses keep dancing. This would be a good way to weed out the weaker people. Dance or die! Natural selection with a beat.

One good result, of course, would be that during the actual dancing, no fighting could take place. But the plan would also tend to reduce violence during the remainder of the year, because for six months following the dance, everyone would be talking about how much fun they had had, and for the six months after that, they would all be busy planning what to wear to next year's dance.

Another plan I have is World Peace Through Formal Introductions. The idea is that everyone in the world would be required to meet everyone else in the world, formally, at least once. You'd have to look the person in the eye, shake hands, repeat their name, and try to remember one outstanding physical characteristic. My theory is, if you knew everyone in the world personally, you'd be less inclined to fight them in a war: "Who? The Malaysians? Are you kidding? I know those people!"

The biggest problem with compulsory, world-wide formal introductions would be logistics. How would it work? Would you line up everyone in the world single file and have one person at a time move down the line meeting all the others? And then when they finish they get on the end of the line, and the next person starts?

Or would you divide everyone into two long lines and have them move past each other laterally? That seems inefficient, because, for at least part of the time, each line would have a large number of people with nothing to do. And also, once you finished the first pass, everyone would still have to meet the people in their own line.

Either way, it would take a very long time. In fact, children would be born during the introductions, and then you'd have to meet them, too.

And it's probably important to remember that because of their longer names, some nationalities would move through the line more slowly than others. Russians, for example. Russian names tend to be long. If you ever bought an ID bracelet for a Russian person, you know what I mean. The engraving alone can run over two hundred dollars.

I'm afraid the Russians would move through the line very slowly: "Vladimir Denisovitch Zhirinovski, this is Yevgeny Vasily Arbatov. Yevgeny Vasily Arbatov, meet Vladimir Denisovitch Zhirinovski." Major delay.

On the other hand, the Chinese tend to have short names. "Chin Lu, Wu Han. Wu Han, Chin Lu." Bing! See ya later! Movin' right along. Which is why there are so many Chinese: less time saying hello, more time to fuck.

Peace on you. But only if you really deserve it.

POLITICALLY CORRECT
LANGUAGE

I know I'm a little late with this, but I'd like to get a few licks in on this bogus topic before it completely disappears from everyone's consciousness.

First, I want to be really clear about one thing: as far as other people's feelings are concerned—especially these "victim groups"—when I deal with them as individuals, I will call them whatever they want. When it's one on one, if some guy wants me to call him a morbidly obese, African-ancestored male with a same-gendered sexual orientation I'll be glad to do that. On the other hand, if he wants me to call him a fat nigger cocksucker, then that's what it will be. I'm here to please.

If I meet a woman who wishes to be referred to as a motion-impaired, same-gender-oriented Italian-American who is difficult to deal with, fine. On the other hand, I am perfectly willing to call her a crippled, Guinea dyke cunt if she prefers. I'm not trying to change anyone's self-image. But! But! When I am speaking generally, and impersonally, about a large group of people, especially these victim groups, I will call them what I think is honest and fair. And I will try not to bullshit myself.

OK, so, who exactly are these victims? Well, first of all, I don't think everyone who says he's a victim automatically qualifies. I don't think a homely, disfigured, bald minority person with a room-temperature IQ who limps and stutters is necessarily always a victim. Although I will say she probably shouldn't be out trying to get work as a receptionist. But maybe that's just the way it oughta be.

I'm more interested in real victims. People who have been chronically and systematically fucked over by the system. Because the United States is a Christian racist nation with a rigged economic system run for three hundred years by the least morally qualified of the two sexes, there were bound to be some real victims. People who've been elaborately fucked over.

The way I see it, this country has only four real victim groups: Indians, blacks, women, and gays. I purposely left out the Spanish and Asians, because when you look at what happened to the Indians and blacks, the Spanish and Asian people have had a walk in the park. It's not even close. Not to downplay the shit they've had to eat, but in about one hundred years the Spanish and Asians are going to be running this country, so they'll have plenty of chances to get even with the gray people.

Let's get to some of these other non-victims. You probably noticed, elsewhere I used the word *fat*. I used that word because that's what fat people are. They're fat. They're not large; they're not stout, chunky, hefty, or plump. And they're not big-boned. Dinosaurs are big-boned. These people are not necessarily obese, either. *Obese* is a medical term. And they're not overweight. Overweight implies there is some correct weight. There is no correct weight. Heavy is also a misleading term. An aircraft carrier is heavy; it's not fat. Only people are fat, and that's what fat people are. They're fat. I offer no apology for this. It is not intended as criticism or insult. It is simply descriptive language. I don't like euphemisms. Euphemisms are a form of lying. Fat people are not gravitationally disadvantaged. They're fat. I prefer seeing things the way they are, not the way some people wish they were.

I don't believe certain groups deserve extra-special names.

For instance, midgets and dwarfs are midgets and dwarfs. They're not little people. Infants are little people; leprechauns are little people. Midgets and dwarfs are midgets and dwarfs. They don't get any taller by calling them little people. I wish their lives were different. I wish they didn't have to walk around staring at other people's crotches, but I can't fix that. And I'm not going to lie about what they are. The politically sensitive language commandos would probably like me to call them "vertically challenged." They're not vertically challenged. A skydiver is vertically challenged. The person who designed the Empire State Building was vertically challenged. Midgets and dwarfs are midgets and dwarfs.

Also, crippled people are crippled, they're not differently-abled. If you insist on using tortured language like differently-abled, then you must include all of us. We're all differently-abled. You can do things I can't do; I can do things you can't do. I can pick my nose with my thumb, and I can switch hands while masturbating and gain a stroke. We're all differently-abled. Crippled people are simply crippled. It's a perfectly honorable word. There is no shame in it. It's in the Bible: "Jesus healed the cripples." He didn't engage in rehabilitative strategies for the physically disadvantaged.

So, leaving aside women and gays for the moment, I've narrowed it down to blacks and Indians. Let's talk about what we ought to call them, and let's talk about what the language commandos would like us to call them. And remember, this has nothing to do with the people themselves. It has to do with the words.

And, by the way, when it comes to these liberal language vandals, I must say I agree with their underlying premise: White Europeans and their descendants are morally unattractive people who are responsible for most of the world's suffering. That part is easy. You would have to be, uh, visually impaired not to see it. The impulse behind political correctness is a good one. But like every good impulse in America it has been grotesquely distorted beyond usefulness.

Clearly, there are victims, but I don't agree that these failed campus revolutionaries know what to do about them. When they're not busy curtailing freedom of speech, they're running around inventing absurd hyphenated names designed to make people feel better. Remember, these are the white elitists in their customary paternalistic role: protecting helpless, inept minority victims. Big Daddy White Boss always knows best.

So, let me tell you how I handle some of these speech issues. First of all, I say "black." I say "black" because most black people prefer "black." I don't say "people of color." People of color sounds like something you see when you're on mushrooms. Besides, the use of people of color is dishonest. It means precisely the same as colored people. If you're not willing to say "colored people," you shouldn't be saying "people of color."

Besides, the whole idea of color is bullshit anyway. What should we call white people? "People of no color"? Isn't pink a color? In fact, white people are not really white at all, they're different shades of pink, olive, and beige. In other words, they're colored. And black people are rarely black. I see mostly different shades of brown and tan. In fact, some light-skinned black people are lighter than the darkest white people. Look how dark the people in India are. They're dark brown, but they're considered white people. What's going on here? May I see the color chart? "People of color" is an awkward, bullshit, liberal-guilt phrase that obscures meaning rather than enhanc-ing it. Shall we call fat people, "people of size"?

By the way, I think the whole reason we're encouraged in this country to think of ourselves as "black and white" (instead of "pink and brown," which is what we are) is that black and white are complete opposites that cannot be reconciled. Black and white can never come together. Pink and brown, on the other hand, might just stand a chance of being blended, might just come together. Can't have that! Doesn't fit the plan.

I also don't say "African-American." I find it completely illogical, and furthermore it's confusing. Which part of Africa are we talking about? What about Egypt? Egypt is in Africa. Egyptians aren't black. They're like the people in India, they're dark brown white people. But they're Africans. So why wouldn't an Egyptian who becomes a U.S. citizen be an African-American?

The same thing goes for the Republic of South Africa. Suppose a white racist from South Africa becomes an American citizen? Well, first of all he'd find plenty of com-pany, but couldn't he also be called an African-American? It seems to me that a racist white South-African guy could come here and call himself African-American just to piss off black people. And, by the way, what about a black person born in South Africa who moves here and becomes a citi-zen? What is he? An African-South-African-American? Or a South-African-African-American?

All right, back to this hemisphere. How about a black woman who is a citizen of Jamaica? According to P.C. doc-trine, she's an African-Jamaican, right? But if she becomes a U.S. citizen, she's a Jamaican-American. And yet if one of these language crusaders saw her on the street, he'd think she was an African-American. Unless he knew her personally in which case he would have to decide between African-Jamaican-American and Jamaican-African-American. Ya know? It's just so much liberal bullshit. Labels divide people. We need fewer labels, not more.

Now, the Indians. I call them Indians because that's what they are. They're Indians. There's nothing wrong with the word *Indian*. First of all, it's important to know that the word *Indian* does not derive from Columbus mistakenly believing he had reached "India." India was not even called by that name in 1492; it was known as Hindustan. More likely, the word *Indian* comes from Columbus's description of the people he found here. He was an Italian, and did not speak or write very good Spanish, so in his written accounts he called the Indians, "Una gente in Dios." A people in God. In God. In Dios. Indians. It's a perfectly noble and respectable word.

So let's look at this pussified, trendy bullshit phrase, Native Americans. First of all, they're not natives. They came over the Bering land bridge from Asia, so they're not natives. There are no natives anywhere in the world. Everyone is from some-where else. All people are refugees, immigrants, or aliens. If there were natives anywhere, they would be people who still live in the Great Rift valley in Africa where the human species arose. Everyone else is just visiting. So much for the "native" part of Native American.

As far as calling them "Americans" is concerned, do I even have to point out what an insult this is? Jesus Holy Shit Christ! We steal their hemisphere, kill twenty or so million* of them, destroy five hundred separate cultures, herd the survivors onto the worst land we can find, and now we want to name them after ourselves? It's appalling. Haven't we done enough

---

* Before 1492 there were 25 million people in Central America. By 1579 there were 2 million.

damage? Do we have to further degrade them by tagging them with the repulsive name of their conquerors?

And as far as these classroom liberals who insist on saying "Native American" are concerned, here's something they should be told: It's not up to you to name people and tell them what they ought to be called. If you'd leave the classroom once in a while, you'd find that most Indians are insulted by the term *Native American*. The American Indian Movement will tell you that if you ask them.

The phrase "Native American" was invented by the U.S. government Department of the Interior in 1970. It is an inventory term used to keep track of people. It includes Hawaiians, Eskimos, Samoans, Micronesians, Polynesians, and Aleuts. Anyone who uses the phrase *Native American* is assisting the U.S. government in its effort to obliterate people's true identities.

Do you want to know what the Indians would like to be called? Their real names: Adirondack, Delaware, Massachuset, Narraganset, Potomac, Illinois, Miami, Alabama, Ottawa, Waco, Wichita, Mohave, Shasta, Yuma, Erie, Huron, Susquehanna, Natchez, Mobile, Yakima, Wallawalla, Muskogee, Spokan, Iowa, Missouri, Omaha, Kansa, Biloxi, Dakota, Hatteras, Klamath, Caddo, Tillamook, Washoe, Cayuga, Oneida, Onondaga, Seneca, Laguna, Santa Ana, Winnebago, Pecos, Cheyenne, Menominee, Yankton, Apalachee, Chinook, Catawba, Santa Clara, Taos, Arapaho, Blackfoot, Blackfeet, Chippewa, Cree, Mohawk, Tuscarora, Cherokee, Seminole, Choctaw, Chickasaw, Comanche, Shoshone, Two Kettle, Sans Arc, Chiricahua, Kiowa, Mescalero, Navajo, Nez Perce, Potawatomi, Shawnee, Pawnee, Chickahominy, Flathead, Santee, Assiniboin, Oglala, Miniconjou, Osage, Crow, Brulé, Hunkpapa, Pima, Zuni, Hopi, Paiute, Creek, Kickapoo, Ojibwa, Shinnicock.

You know, you'd think it would be a fairly simple thing to come over to this continent, commit genocide, eliminate the forests, dam up the rivers, build our malls and massage parlors, sell our blenders and whoopee cushions, poison ourselves with chemicals, and let it go at that. But no. We have to compound the insult. Native Americans! I'm glad the Indians have gambling casinos now. It makes me happy that dimwitted white people are losing their rent money to the Indians. Maybe the Indians will get lucky and win their country back. Probably they wouldn't want it. Look what we did to it.

SHORT TAKES (PART 1)

The wisest man I ever knew taught me something I never forgot. And although I never forgot it, I never quite memorized it either. So what I'm left with is the memory of having learned something very wise that I can't quite remember.

Just what exactly is the "old dipsy doodle"?

*When I hear a person talking about political solutions,
I know I am not listening to a serious person.*

Sties are caused by watching your dog shit.

> **SOMETIMES A LITTLE BRAIN DAMAGE CAN HELP**

**A woman told me her child was autistic,
and I thought she said artistic. So I said, "Oh, great.
I'd like to see some of the things he's done."**

Eventually there will come a time when everyone is in a band.

Weyerhauser, a company that makes its money by cutting down trees, calls itself "The tree-growing company."

**If a man smiles all the time he's
probably selling something that doesn't work.**

Not only do I not know what's going on,
I wouldn't know what to do about it if I did.

How likely is it that all the people who are described
as missing are living together in a small town somewhere?

We're all fucked. It helps to remember that.

If lobsters looked like puppies, people could never
drop them in boiling water while they're still alive. But
instead, they look like science fiction monsters, so it's OK.
Restaurants that allow patrons to select live lobsters from
a tank should be made to paint names on their shells:
"Happy," "Baby Doll," "Junior." I defy anyone to drop a
living thing called "Happy" in rapidly boiling water.

The nicest thing about anything is not knowing what it is.

I feel sorry for homeless gay people; they have no closet
to come out of. In fact, I imagine if you *were* gay and homeless,
you'd probably be glad just to *have* a closet.

I've adopted a new lifestyle that doesn't require
my presence. In fact, if I don't want to, I don't have
to get out of bed at all, and I still get credit for a full day.

The sicker you get, the harder it is to remember
if you took your medicine.

I can't bear to go to the children's zoo. I always wonder how
their parents can allow them to be kept in those little cages.

If you take the corn off the cob, not only do you have corn-off-
the-cob, you also have cobs-out-from-inside-the-corn.

Why do foreign soldiers march funny? Do they think we march
funny? If we do, how would we know?

If you mail a letter to the post office, who delivers it?

"On the fritz" is a useful expression only if you're talking about a home appliance. You wouldn't say, "The Space Shuttle is on the fritz." You'd never hear it in a hospital. "Doctor, the heart-lung machine is on the fritz."

Rarely does a loose woman have a tight pussy.

Some see the glass as half-empty, some see the glass as half-full. I see the glass as too big.

My uncle thought he would clean up in dirt farming, but prices fell, and he took a real bath. Eventually, he washed his hands of the whole thing.

Kilometers are shorter than miles.
Save gas, take your next trip in kilometers.

Test of metal: Will of iron, nerves of steel, heart of gold, balls of brass.

WHITE PEOPLE FUCKED UP THE BLUES

If you love someone, set them free; if they come home, set them on fire.

I've never owned a telescope, but it's something I'm thinking of looking into.

Whenever I see a large crowd, I always wonder what was the most disgusting thing any one of them ever did.

*I think they ought to let guys like Jeffrey Dahmer off with
a warning. They do it with speeding tickets. Sometimes
all a guy needs is a good talking to. Why don't they say,
"Listen, Jeff. Knock it off! Nobody thinks you're funny.
Eat one more guy and we're comin' after ya."*

Hey kids! It's mostly bullshit and garbage, and none of the stuff
they tell you is true. And when your dumb-ass father says he
wants you to amount to something, he means make a lot of
money. How do you think the word *amount* got in there?

**Those nicotine patches seem to work pretty well,
but I understand it's kind of hard to keep 'em lit.**

*In El Salvador, they declared a cease fire after ten
years. Why didn't they think of that at the beginning?
Anyway, the best thing about El Salvador is that they
killed a lot of religious people. How often do you get
10 percent of the body count in clergy?*

At one point in my haste to improve myself, I mixed up the
telephone numbers of the Schick Center for the Control of
Smoking and the Evelyn Wood Speed Reading School. As a
result, I can now smoke up to 300 cigarettes a minute, but
I gave up reading.

**"Preschool teacher": If it's not a school, why do they
need a teacher? Don't they need a "preteacher"?**

Most people are not particularly good at anything.

How can someone be "armed with a handgun"? Shouldn't
he be armed with an "armgun"? Can a handgun really be a
sidearm? And shouldn't a hand grenade be an arm grenade?
You don't throw it with your hand, you throw it with your arm.

Try explaining Hitler to a kid.

*Why do we turn lights "out" when we turn
most other things "off"?*

The straightest line between a short distance is two points.

**Working-class people "look for work." Middle-class people "try to
get a job." Upper-middle-class people "seek employment."**

*Can you have just one antic? How about
a lone shenanigan? A monkeyshine?*

There are two pips in a beaut, four beauts in a lulu, eight lulus
in a doozy, and sixteen doozies in a humdinger. No one knows
how many humdingers there are in a lollapalooza.

It is a sad thing to see an Indian wearing a cowboy hat.

*Those who dance are considered insane
by those who can't hear the music.*

THERE WILL BE NO MORE PAPER TOWELS AFTER JULY

It is impossible to know accurately how you look in your sunglasses.

As he ages, Mickey Rooney gets even shorter.

*Elevators and escalators do more than elevate and escalate.
They also lower. The names tell only half the story.*

No one ever refers to "half a month."

**Don't you get discouraged each morning when you
wake up and realize you have to wash again?**

*You show me the people who control the money, the land,
and the weapons, and I'll show you the people in charge.*

I'm not going to apologize for this, but I have my own personal
psychic. He doesn't predict the future, and he can't tell you much
about your past. But he does a really fantastic job of describing
the present. For instance, he can tell you exactly what you're
wearing, but he can't do it over the phone.

**We're all amateurs; it's just that some of us
are more professional about it than others.**

When the going gets tough, the tough get fucked.

I was expelled from cooking school,
and it left a bad taste in my mouth.

**Last year, in Los Angeles, a robber threatened a store owner with a
syringe that he claimed had HIV on it, saying "Give me the money or
I'll give you AIDS." You know what I would've told him? "If you give
me AIDS I'm gonna find your wife and daughter and fuck them."**

I think we should attack Russia now. They'd never expect it.

I have as much authority as the Pope, I just don't have
as many people who believe it.

What is the plural of "a hell of a guy"? "Hells of guys"?

The phrase surgical strike *might be more acceptable if it were
common practice to perform surgery with high explosives.*

I never eat sushi. I have trouble eating things that are merely
unconscious.

When you find existing time on a parking meter, you should be able to add it to the end of your life. Minus the time you spent on hold.

I recently went to a new doctor and noticed he was located in something called the Professional Building. I felt better right away.

You can't fight City Hall, but you can goddamn sure blow it up.

Just think, right now as you read this, some guy somewhere is gettin' ready to hang himself.

JESUS WAS A CROSS-DRESSER

I have no ax to grind, but I do have an ivory letter opener that could use sharpening.

Feminists want to ban pornography on the grounds that it encourages violence against women. The Japanese consume far more violent and depraved pornography than we do, and yet there is almost no rape reported there. A woman is twenty times more in danger of being raped in the U.S. than she is in Japan. Why? Because Japanese people are decent, civilized, and intelligent.

The only good thing ever to come out of religion was the music.

I don't have to tell you it goes without saying there are some things better left unsaid. I think that speaks for itself. The less said about it the better.

Do kings have sweat bands in their crowns?

When someone is impatient and says, "I haven't got all day," I always wonder, How can that be? How can you not have all day?

There ought to be at least one round state.

For a long time it was all right for a woman to keep
a diary, but it sounded too fruity for men. So they changed
it to *journal*. Now sensitive men can set down their thoughts
without appearing *too* sensitive.

In comic strips the person on the left always speaks first.

A courtesy bus driver once told me to go fuck myself.

Sometimes the label on the can says "fancy peas." Then, you get
'em home and they're really rather ordinary. Nothing fancy about
'em, at all. Maybe if they had little bullfight paintings on them, they
would be fancy. But as it is . . .

SLAP A DEAD PERSON

If the shoe fits, get another one just like it.

*Eventually, nature will produce a species
that can play the piano better than we can.*

I don't think we really gave barbarism a fair try.

**Piano lessons sound like something a piano should take.
Humans should take piano-playing lessons.**

*Did you hear about the man who left in a huff and
returned in a jiffy? Another day, he arrived in a tizzy
and left in a snit. His wife swept in in a fury and left in
a daze, then left in a dither and returned in a whirl.*

If you go to a bone bank, why can't you make a calcium deposit?

**"Get down!" is a slang expression that would have been
really useful in World War II. If soldiers had known this
expression at the time, a lot of lives could have been saved.**

WHY CAN'T THERE BE MORE SUFFERING?

There are no times that don't have moments like these.

Since 1983, more than thirty people have been killed in post office shootings. You know why? Because the price of stamps keeps changing. There's a lot of pressure. "How much are they now, Rob? Twenty-nine? Thirty-two? I can't keep track! Fuck it!" BANG BANG BANG BANG BANG BANG BANG BANG BANG!!!

On Opening Day, the President doesn't throw *out* the first ball. He throws it *in*. If he threw it out, it would land in the parking lot and someone would have to go get it.

Where does the dentist go when he leaves you alone?

Why are there never any really good-looking women on long distance buses?

I almost don't feel the way I do.

We're not satisfied with forcing Russia to destroy its nuclear weapons and recant its ideology. Now we're really going to get even: we're sending experts to show them how to run their economy. Am I missing something? A country with a five-trillion-dollar debt is giving advice on handling money?

She "took him to the cleaners." Whenever I hear that I wonder if that was the only errand he had to run. Maybe she also took him to the adult bookstore.

I go to bed early. My favorite dream comes on at nine.

"Best seller" really only means "good seller." There can only be one best seller. All the rest are good sellers. Each succeeding book on the list is a "better seller."

There should be some things we don't name, just so we can sit around all day and wonder what they are.

Everything is still the same. It's just a little different now.

The symphony orchestra had played poorly, so the conductor was in a bad mood. That night he beat his wife—because the music hadn't been beautiful enough.

You know why I stopped eating processed foods?
I began to picture the people who might be processing them.

Whenever I see a large crowd I always think of all the dry cleaning they have out.

I didn't wash today. I wasn't dirty. If I'm not dirty, I don't wash. Some weeks I don't have to shower at all. I just groom my three basic areas: teeth, hair, and asshole. And to save time, I use the same brush.

I AM NOT IN COMPLIANCE

When you buy a six-foot dildo, and call it a marital aid, you are stretching not just the anatomy, but the limits of credibility.

At a formal dinner party, the person nearest death should always be seated closest to the bathroom.

The child molester skipped breakfast, but said he'd grab a little something on the way to work.

THINGS YOU DON'T WANT TO HEAR: "Jeff? We're going to have to break your skull again and reset it. Okay? It's way out of line. It looks really strange. But we won't do it until we've opened up that incision and put some more fire ants inside of you. OK?"

In Panama, during the election that defeated Noriega,
there were "dignity battalions" that wandered the streets
beating and robbing and killing people.

*Someone said to me, "Make yourself a sandwich." Well, if
I could make myself a sandwich, I wouldn't make myself a
sandwich. I'd make myself a horny, 18-year-old billionaire.*

Why would anyone want to use a flood light? I should
think lights would be kind of dangerous during a flood.
Better just to sit in the dark and wait for help.

There are nights when the wolves are silent,
and only the moon howls.

*The nicest thing about a plane crashing at an air show
is that they always have good video of the actual crash.*

How come none of these boxers seem to have a losing record?

Where ideas are concerned, America can be counted on to do
one of two things: take a good idea and run it completely into the
ground, or take a bad idea and run it completely into the ground.

*If I only had one tooth, I think
I would brush it a real long time.*

If we could just find out who's in charge, we could kill him.

Whenever I hear that someone works in his shirtsleeves,
I always wonder what he did with the rest of the shirt.

It is impossible to dry one hand.

The word *bipartisan* usually means some
larger-than-usual deception is being carried out.

I saw an old woman who I thought was looking
on the ground for a contact lens. As I drew closer, I realized
she was actually all hunched over from osteoporosis.

> GERMS LIVE IN MY HAT

*You can lead a gift horse to water in the middle of the stream,
but you can't look him in the mouth and make him drink.*

Deep Throat: Think about it. There is actually an important
figure in American history who is named for a blow-job movie.
How do grade-school teachers handle this?

Regarding the fitness craze: America has lost its soul;
now it's trying to save its body.

*Nothing is so boring as listening to
someone else describe a dream.*

What is all this stuff about a kick being "partially blocked"?
It's either blocked, not blocked, or deflected. Partially blocked
is like "somewhat dead."

I notice I don't see as many buck-toothed women as I used to.

*The thing I like the most about this country is that,
in a pinch, when things really get tough, you can
always go into a store and buy some mints.*

I've watched so many documentaries about World War II,
I'm sure I've seen the same people die hundreds of times.

I'll bet there aren't too many people hooked on crack
who can play the bagpipes.

I read that some guy was giving up the governor's chair to run
for a Senate seat. Why would he give up a chair to run for a
seat? Why not be a judge and sit on the bench?

How do primitive people know if they're doing the dances correctly?

THINGS YOU NEVER HEAR:
"Please stop sucking my dick or I'll call the police."

Regarding smoking in public: Suppose you were eating
in a restaurant, and every two minutes the guy at the
next table threw some anthrax germs in the air. Wouldn't
you want to sit in a different section?

The savings-and-loan associations that will cost
$500 billion to bail out are called "the thrifts."

The idea of a walk-in closet sounds frightening. If I'm ever sittin'
at home and a closet walks in, I'm gettin' outta there.

The reason they call it the American Dream is
because you have to be asleep to believe it.

I'D RATHER BE COMING

How can there possibly be a self-addressed envelope? They say now
they even have envelopes that are self-sealing. This I gotta see!

I saw a sign: Park and ride. It's confusing.
They really oughta make up their minds.

Park and lock. Here we go again. If you park and lock, you're
stuck in the car. It should be park, get out, and lock.

"No comment" is a comment.

Why is it like this? Why isn't everything different?

If you have chicken at lunch and chicken at dinner,
do you ever wonder if the two chickens knew each other?

She was only a prostitute, but she had
the nicest face I ever came across.

It's odd that the word *breath* becomes *breathe* by adding
a letter at the end, and yet the pronunciation changes in the
middle. And *woman* becomes *women* by changing the vowel at the
end, while the pronunciation changes near the beginning.
Was somebody drunk when these decisions were made?

Russia actually has something called vodka riots.

I think it would be fun to go on *Jeopardy* and never buzz in. Just
stand there for half an hour, never talk, and then go home.

Diplomatic immunity is necessary, because of the many diseases
diplomats are exposed to in foreign countries.

Why is San Francisco in the "bay area," but Saudi Arabia is
in the "gulf region"? Is a region really bigger than an area?

Whenever I hear about a spy ring, I always wonder if that's the only
jewelry they wear. You'd think a spy wouldn't want to call attention
to himself with a lot of flashy jewelry. For instance, you never hear
about a spy necklace.

> **THIS IS JUST SOME PRINTING**

It's better if an entire family gets Alzheimer's disease.
That way they can all sit around and wonder who they are.

Time sharing got a bad name,
so now they call it "interval ownership."

Harness racing may be all right for some people,
but I prefer watching the horses.

If you get cheated by the Better Business Bureau,
who do you complain to?

As soon as a person tells you they have a surprise
for you, they have lost the element of surprise.

I saw a picture of the inventor of the hydrogen bomb,
Edward Teller, wearing a tie clip. Why would the man who
invented a bomb that destroys everything for fifty miles be
concerned about whether or not his tie was straight?

No one calls you "Bub" anymore.

Why is there such controversy about drug testing?
I know plenty of guys who'd be willing to test
any drug they can come up with.

If the Cincinnati Reds were really the first
major league baseball team, who did they play?

I AM REPELLED BY WHOLESOMENESS

When they say someone is making a "personal tour,"
are they suggesting that, on the other hand, it is somehow
possible to make a tour without actually being there?

*After how much time does a
persistent cough become a chronic cough?*

Intelligence tests are biased toward the literate.

**The carousel and Ferris wheel owners traveled in
different circles so they rarely made the rounds together.**

Which is more immoral? Killing two 100-pound people
or killing one 300-pound person?

**Guest host is a bad enough oxymoron, but NBC raised the stakes
when, a few years back, they installed Jay Leno as the "permanent
guest host." Not to be outdone, Joan Rivers pointed out that she had
been the "first permanent guest host." Check, please!**

I don't own a camera, so I travel with a police sketch artist.

If JFK Jr. got into a taxi in New York to go to the airport, do you
think he would say, "Take me to JFK?" How would he feel about
that? And how does Lee Harvey Oswald's mother feel when she
walks through JFK, knowing that if she had stayed single it
would probably be Martin Luther King Jr. Airport?

Which is taller, a short-order cook or a small-engine mechanic?

Hobbies are for people who lack direction.

> **FUCK SOCCER MOMS**

A graveyard always has to start with a single body. Unless the local
people get lucky and there's a nice big bus accident in town.

**A lot of times when they catch a guy who killed twenty-seven people,
they say, "He was a loner." Well, of course he was a loner;
he killed everyone he came in contact with.**

Is it illegal to charge admission to a free-for-all?

I read about some mob guy who was being charged with
gambling, loan sharking, extortion, narcotics, prostitution, murder,
pornography, labor racketeering, stolen cars, business fraud, mail
fraud, wire fraud, bribery, corruption, perjury, and jury tampering.
Here's a guy who didn't waste a minute. Busy, busy, busy!

My definition of bad luck: catching AIDS from a Quaker.

Dogs and cats get put to sleep,
hogs and cows get slaughtered.

If a speed freak went to Rapid City to make a quick buck
in fast food he might sell instant coffee in an express lane.

I worry about my judgment when anything I believe in or do
regularly begins to be accepted by the American public.

Imagine how thick Japanese people's photo albums must be.

Some national parks have long waiting lists for camping
reservations. I think when you have to wait a year to sleep
next to a tree, something is wrong.

When football fans tear down the goalpost, where do they take it?

Just because your penis surgery was not successful
is no reason to go off half-cocked.

In England in 1830, William Huskisson became the first person ever
run over by a railroad train. Wouldn't that make you feel stupid?
For millions and millions of years there were no trains, and then
suddenly they have trains and you get run over?

NOTHING RHYMES WITH NOSTRIL

**Shouldn't a complimentary beverage tell you
what a fine person you are?**

*Only Americans could find as a prime means of
self-expression the wave and the high five.*

It is important to remember that although the Automobile Club
has a health plan, the health club does not have an automobile plan.

Auto racing: slow minds and fast cars.

*If you fuck a baseball player's wife while he's
on the road, his team will lose the next day.*

If Helen Keller had psychic ability, would you
say she had a fourth sense?

**Why do the Dutch people have two names for their country, Holland
and the Netherlands, and neither one includes the word *Dutch*?**

*Late one night it struck me that for several years
I had been masturbating to a Wilma Flintstone fantasy.*

Why do we say redheaded but brownhaired?

**Does the water that signifies the passage of time flow under
the bridge, or over the dam? I've heard both versions, and I'm
concerned about the people who live near the dam.**

*In the movies, when someone buys something
they never wait for their change.*

I buy stamps by mail. It works OK until I run out of stamps.

**Whenever someone tells me they're going to fix a chicken, I always
think, Maybe it isn't really broken. Maybe it just needs a little oil.**

My only superstition: if you drop a spoon,
a wild pig will offer to finance your next car.

As a matter of principle I never attend the first annual anything.

Why is it with any piece of home electronics equipment
there are always a few buttons and switches you never use?

There is actually a show on the Lifetime
channel called "Dentistry Update."

When you eat two different types of candy bars in succession,
the second one is not as easy to enjoy because you get
so used to how good the first one tastes.

BLOOD IS THICKER THAN URINE

They said some guy arrested for murder in Las Vegas
had "a history of questionable actions." Can you imagine
if we were all held to that standard?

There is no will, and there is no wisdom.

Some people like to watch "monster trucks" drive on top of cars
and crush them. Then there are the other people who
can't get to the arena, because they don't have cars.

A lot of these people who keep a gun at home for safety
are the same ones who refuse to wear a seat belt.

It's legal for men to be floorwalkers and illegal
for women to be streetwalkers.

Look at the self-help titles in the bookstore, and you'll get a fews clues about our culture. They're all about aggression and acquisition. It wouldn't be at all surprising to see a book called *How to Force Your Will on Other People by Giving Them the Shaft and Fucking Them out of Their Money*.

When you sneeze, all the numbers in your head go up by one.

How can crash course and collision course have two different meanings?

I wanted to get a job as a gynecologist, but I couldn't find an opening.

Why don't they have dessert at breakfast?

Sometimes I look out the airplane window at a large city at night and wonder how many people are fucking.

Why don't they have rye pancakes? Grapefruit cookies? Fig ice cream? Canteloupe pie?

The *mai tai* got its name when two Polynesian alcoholics got in a fight over some neckwear.

I hope they do clone the dinosaurs, and they come back just in time for the ozone layer to disappear and wipe those ugly motherfuckers out again.

In most polls there are always about 5 percent of the people who "don't know." What isn't generally understood is that it's the same people in every poll.

I read that a patient got AIDS from his dentist. It wasn't from the blood; apparently, the dentist fucked him in the ass. "Open wide!"

Regarding Red Riding Hood: Wolves can't be all bad if they'll eat your grandmother. Even Grandpa won't do that.

I think we've outgrown the word *gripe*. When everyone has automatic weapons, a word like *gripe* is sort of irrelevant.

PIG SNERV

**"The friendly skies." "The skies are not cloudy."
How is this possible? I look up, I see one sky.**

Kids are now being born with syphilis and cocaine habits. There's nothing like waking up your second day on Earth and realizing that once you kick cocaine you're still gonna have the syph. And hey, kids! If you didn't get VD in the womb, don't worry, you still have a shot. Some toddlers recently picked up gonorrhea at a day care center.

I always thought a semi-truck driver was someone who dropped out of truck-driving school halfway through the course.

**When Sammy Davis Jr. kissed a woman,
do you think he closed his bad eye?**

Environmentalists changed the word jungle *to* rain forest, *because no one would give them money to save a jungle. Same with* swamps *and* wetlands.

When a lion escapes from a circus in Africa, how do they know when they've caught the right one?

**The safest place to be during an earthquake
would be in a stationary store.**

*Wouldn't it be funny if you went to group therapy
and the Mills Brothers were there?*

I'm not an organ donor, but I once gave
an old piano to the Salvation Army.

Cancer research is a growth industry.

*Sometimes I sit for hours weighing the fine distinctions
among* spunk, pluck, balls, nerve, chutzpah, gall, *and* moxie.

It is impossible for an abortion clinic to have
a waiting list of more than nine months.

> **YOU NEVER SEE A SMILING RUNNER**

**Carjackings, smash-and-grabs, snipers, home invasions,
follow-home robberies, hostage incidents, barricade/standoff
situations, drive-by shootings, walk-up shootings, traffic shootings,
pipe bombs, mail bombs. Shit! We never had cool crimes like that
when I was a kid. All we had was robbery and murder. I feel deprived.**

*In a hotel, why can't you use
the house phone to phone your house?*

I'm bringing out my own line of colognes. You've heard of
Eternity, Obsession, and Passion? Mine is Stench! I'm offering
a choice of five fragrances: Bait Shop, Animal Waste, Landfill,
Human Remains, and Chemical Toilet.

**When I was a kid I used to think it was
all the same clouds that kept coming by.**

SOMETHING IS DREADFULLY WRONG IN THIS COUNTRY:
There is now an "empathy breast." It is a wrap-around vest
that has a pocket for placing the baby's bottle in. The new
father wears it while "nursing" the baby. Jesus!

Sometimes on a rainy day I sit around and
weed the losers out of my address book.

**They said on the news that tests on monkeys showed HIV
can be transmitted through oral sex. What I want to know is,
who had to blow the monkeys?**

The other night I ate at a real nice family restaurant.
Every table had an argument going.

I don't live in the fast lane, but have you ever seen
one of those cars parked on the median with its hood up?

**Just think, right now, all over the world there are people
exercising bad judgment. Somebody, right this minute,
is probably making the mistake of his life.**

Poor confetti. Its useful life lasts about two seconds.
And it can never be used again.

Human beings are kind of interesting from birth until they reach
the age of a year and a half. Then they are boring until they reach
fifty. By that time they're either completely defeated and fucked up,
which makes them interesting again, or they've learned how to beat
the game, and that makes them interesting, too.

THINK OFF-CENTER

The older I get, the more certain I am that I will not
have to spend the rest of my life in prison.

Assisted suicide is controversial. There are moral, medical,
legal, and ethical arguments. But the truth of it is,
a lot of people just want to get the fuck outta here.

*What exactly do you do when the Dalai Lama appears on
"Nightline," and you're not satisfied with his answers?*

Whenever I see a picture of a group of people in the newspaper,
I always wonder how many of them have had really depraved sex
since the picture was taken.

A small town is any place too poor
to have its own insane asylum.

*Texas canceled plans to put its motto, Friendship, on its
license plates. People complained that it was too wimpy. Why
don't they just change their motto? Let's Kill All the Niggers
comes to mind as appropriate.*

In Vienna, they recently had an opera riot.

Never get on an airplane if the pilot is wearing a hat that has more
than three pastel colors.

*Why is it when you buy five shirts, there's always one you
never wear? To minimize this problem, when I shop for shirts I
always put one back just before I pay.*

My family and I are doing our bit for the environment. We've
volunteered to have sixty metric tons of human waste stored in our
home.

> CANCER CAUSES HEART DISEASE

Shopping and buying and getting and having comprise
the Great American Addiction. No one is immune: When the
underclass riots in this country, they don't kill policemen and
politicians, they steal merchandise. How embarrassing.

I made a bargain with the devil: I would get to be famous,
and he would get to fuck my sister.

Granola bars didn't sell very well when they were good for you. Now
they have caramel, chocolate, marshmallow, saturated fat, and
sweeteners; and a small amount of oats and wheat. Sales picked up.

You know you're in trouble when you look behind the clerk and see
one of your personal checks displayed on the wall as an example of
why the store does not accept personal checks.

As grown-ups, we never get to "wave bye-bye." I think it
would be fun. "Steve, the boss is sailing for Europe; we're all
going down to the dock to wave bye-bye."

Some things a king never has to say:
"Can I play, too?"
"Hey, guys, wait for me."
"I never seem to get laid."

Did you ever go somewhere and realize it used to be a different
place? And it dawns on you that some things are not here anymore.
Of course, some other things are not here *yet*. And nothing seems
to be where it used to be; everything's been moved. Sometimes
I think if we could just put everything back where it
originally was, we might be all right.

I was surprised when I started getting old. I always thought it was one of those things that would happen to someone else.

> **ALUMINUM IS A JIVE METAL**

You know you're in a poor neighborhood when you give the store clerk a dollar and he asks you if you have anything smaller.

Since childhood is a time when kids prepare to be grown-ups, I think it makes a lot of sense to completely traumatize your children. Gets 'em ready for the real world.

With all that humping going on, JFK's administration shouldn't have been called Camelot, they should have called it Come-a-lot.

There is a new British rock band called So Long, Mate! During each performance one member of the band is ritually slaughtered. The music has a certain urgency, but the tours are nice and short. About five days.

When the convention of testicle transplant surgeons had its annual softball game, they asked me to throw out the first ball.

You know what would be fun? Drop acid, smoke PCP, and then take the White House tour with Jim Carrey.

I don't believe there's any problem in this country, no matter how tough it is, that Americans, when they roll up their sleeves, can't completely ignore.

Sometimes a fireman will go to great, strenuous lengths to save a raccoon that's stuck in a drainpipe and then go out on the weekend and kill several of them for amusement.

They debated the NAFTA trade bill for a long time; should we sign it or not? Either way, the people get fucked. Trade always exists for the traders. Anytime you hear businessmen debating "which policy is better for America," don't bend over.

Property is theft. Nobody owns anything. When you die, it stays here. I read about these billionaires: Sam Walton 20 billion, Daniel Ludwig 15 billion. They're both dead. They're gone, and the money is still here. It wasn't their money to begin with. Property is theft.

If you want to keep your dog in line, walk him past the fur shop a couple of times a week.

There are only two places in the world: over here and over there.

MILK CHOCOLATE IS FOR SCHMUCKS

I have a photograph of Judge Bork, but it doesn't do him justice.

Have you ever wondered why Republicans are so interested in encouraging people to volunteer in their communities? It's because volunteers work for no pay. Republicans have been trying to get people to work for no pay for a long time.

I finally accepted Jesus. Not as my personal savior, but as a man I intend to borrow money from.

It used to be, cars had cool names: Dart, Hawk, Fury, Cougar, Firebird, Hornet, Mustang, Barracuda. Rocket 88! Now we have Elantra, Altima, Acura, Lumina, Sentra, Corolla, Maxima. Tercel! What the fuck kind of lifeless, pussy names are these? Further proof America has lost its edge.

I'm starting a campaign to have Finland removed as a country. We don't need it.

What a spot! You're in surgery, the anesthetic wears off, and as you wake up you realize that someone in surgical clothing is carrying one of your legs over to a garbage can. The surgeon, holding a large power saw, says, "We're all out of anesthetic, but if you'll hold on real tight to the sides of that gurney, I'll have that other leg off in a jiffy."

You rarely meet a wino with perfect pitch.

Although the photographer and the art thief were close friends, neither had ever taken the other's picture.

Traditional American values: Genocide, aggression, conformity, emotional repression, hypocrisy, and the worship of comfort and consumer goods.

I read that Domino's Pizza trucks have killed more than twenty people. And that's not counting the ones who eat the pizza.

I like it when a flower or a little tuft of grass grows through a crack in the concrete. It's so fuckin' heroic.

A group of cult people has emerged who not only believe Elvis Presley is alive, but have decided that if they find him they will kill and skin him.

There are ten thousand people in the United States in a persistent vegetative state. Just enough to start a small town. Think of them as veggie-burghers.

Apparently, the Hells Angels are suing a movie producer because they said his film shows disrespect for the Hells Angels. OK.

SIMON SAYS, GO FUCK YOURSELF

SOMETHING IS DREADFULLY WRONG IN THIS COUNTRY:
There is actually an organization called Wrestlers Against Drugs,
and on TV there is now a Christian weight-lifting tour.

> **I once read that in Lebanon a peacekeeping force
> was attacked by a religious militia. They deserve each other.**

> *Ross Perot. Just what a nation
> of idiots needs: a short, loud idiot.*

When you visualize the recent past, do you see it
as being somewhere over on the left?

> **Now the brainless New Age spiritual zombies are using bulldozers
> to vandalize the Ouachita National Forest in Arkansas in search of
> crystals. Nothing like that being-in-harmony-with-nature shit.**

> *In some places, a seventeen-year-old girl needs
> a note for being absent from school,
> but she does not need one to get an abortion.*

There's a moment coming. It's not here yet.
It's still on the way. It's in the future. It hasn't arrived.
Here it comes. Here it is . . . shit! It's gone.

> **A sure way to cure hiccups is to jam your fist down
> the affected person's throat and quickly open and close
> your hand several times. It relaxes the vega nerve.**

> *SOMETHING IS DREADFULLY WRONG IN THIS COUNTRY:
> In a November 1990 Gallup Poll of 1,108 Americans,
> 78 percent said they believed there was a place where people
> who had led good lives were eternally rewarded, and
> 60 percent believed there was a place where those who
> led bad lives and died without repentance were
> eternally damned. I find this profoundly disturbing.*

I always order the International Breakfast: French toast, English muffin, Belgian waffle, Spanish omelet, Danish pastry, Swedish pancakes, Canadian bacon, and Irish Coffee.

THERE ARE GHOSTS IN MY SINUSES

Regarding local residents attempting to ban sex shops from their neighborhoods: You show me a parent who says he's worried about his child's innocence, and I'll show you a homeowner trying to maintain equity.

I thought it would be nice to get a job at a duty-free shop, but it doesn't sound like there's a whole lot to do in a place like that.

There's an odd feeling you get when someone on the sidewalk moves slightly to avoid walking into you. It proves you exist. Your mere existence caused them to alter their path. It's a nice feeling. After you die, no one has to get out of your way anymore.

Instead of school busing and prayer in schools, which are both controversial, why not a joint solution? Prayer in buses. Just drive these kids around all day and let them pray their fuckin' empty little heads off.

Lorena Bobbitt only did what men do to each other all the time: She showed an asshole she meant business.

Americans are fucked. They've been bought off. And they came real cheap: a few million dirt bikes, camcorders, microwaves, cordless phones, digital watches, answering machines, jet skis, and sneakers with lights in them. You say you want a few items back from the Bill of Rights? Just promise the doofuses new gizmos.

I love it in a movie when they throw a guy off a cliff. I love it even when it's not a movie. No, especially when it's not a movie.

*Owing to a basic programming flaw,
many computer calculations, including mortgages and
pensions, will be thrown off by the arrival of the year 2000.
It's because many computer programs use only the
last two digits for calculating years. It will cost between
50 and 100 billion dollars to correct this mistake.
I'm glad. I like anything that causes trouble.*

Men don't show emotion, except rage, because it takes strength
to show soft emotions. Most men don't have that kind of strength.
They keep things inside. Then they kill someone.

**Regarding Mount Rushmore: The Black Hills are
sacred Indian ground. Imagine the creepy feeling of four
leering European faces staring at your ancestors for eternity.**

*Who are all these people whose eyeglasses are attached
to straps and bands around their necks? Please! Folks.
Too precious. Hold your glasses, or set them down like
the rest of us. Or perhaps, strange as it sounds, put them on.
You need a dual correction? Get some bifocals.*

THE PLANET IS FINE, THE PEOPLE ARE FUCKED

At some point, during every stage show I do, I take a sip of water and ask the audience, "How's the water here?" I haven't gotten a positive response yet. Not one. Last year I was in 100 different cities. Not one audience was able to give me a positive answer. Nobody trusts their water supply. Nobody.

And that amuses me. Because it means the system is beginning to collapse, beginning to break down. I enjoy chaos and disorder. Not just because they help me professionally; they're also my hobby. I'm an entropy buff.

In high school, when I first heard of entropy, I was attracted to it immediately. They said that in nature all systems are breaking down, and I thought, What a wonderful thing; perhaps I can make some small contribution to this process, myself. And, of course, it's not just true of nature, it's true of society as well. If you look carefully, you can see that the social structure is just beginning to break down, just beginning to come apart at the seams.

The News Turns *Me* On

What I like about that is that it makes the news on television more exciting. I watch the news for only one thing: entertainment. That's all I want. You know my favorite thing on television? Bad news. Accidents, disasters, catastrophes, explosions, fires. I wanna see shit being destroyed and bodies flyin' around.

I'm not interested in the budget, I don't care about tax negotiations, I don't wanna know what country the pope is in. But show me a burning hospital with people on crutches jumpin' off the roof, and I'm a happy guy. I wanna see a paint factory blowin' up, an oil refinery explode, and a tornado hit a church on Sunday. I wanna be told there's a guy runnin' through the Kmart shooting at customers with an automatic weapon. I wanna see thousands of people in the street killing policemen; hear about a nuclear meltdown in a big city; find out the stock market dropped 4,000 points in one day. I wanna see people under pressure!

Sirens, flames, smokes, bodies, graves being filled, parents weeping. My kinda TV! Exciting shit! I just want some entertainment! That's the kind of guy I am. You know what I like most? Big chunks of steel, concrete, and fiery wood falling out of the sky, and people running around trying to get out of the way. Exciting shit!

Fuck Pakistan!

At least I admit it. Most people won't admit those feelings. Most people see somethin' like that, they say, "Ohhhh, isn't that awful?" Bullshit! Lyin' asshole! You love it and you know it. Explosions are fun. And the closer the explosion is to your house, the more fun it is. Have you ever noticed that?

Sometimes an announcer comes on television and says, "Six thousand people were killed in an explosion today." You say, "Where, where?" He says, "In Pakistan." You say, "Aww, fuck Pakistan. Too far away to be fun." But if he says it happened in your hometown, you say, "Whooa, hot shit, Dave! C'mon! Let's go down and look at the bodies!"

I love bad news. Doesn't bother me. The more bad news there is, the faster this system collapses. I'm glad the water sucks. You know what I do about it? I drink it! I fuckin' drink it!

This Is One Bad Species

You see, I'm not one of those people who worries about everything. Do you have people around you like that? The country's full of 'em now. People walkin' around all day, worried about everything. Worried about the air, the water, the soil, pesticides, food additives, carcinogens, radon, asbestos. Worried about saving endangered species.

Lemme tell you about endangered species. Saving endangered species is just one more arrogant human attempt to control nature. That's what got us in trouble in the first place. Interfering with nature. Meddling. Doesn't anybody understand that?

And as far as endangered species are concerned, it's a phony issue. Over 90 percent of all the species that ever lived on this planet are gone. They're extinct. We didn't kill them; they just disappeared. That's what species do: they appear, and they disappear. It's nature's way. Irrespective of our behavior, species vanish at the rate of twenty-five a day. Let them go gracefully. Stop interfering. Leave nature alone. Haven't we done enough damage?

We're so self-important. So arrogant. Everybody's going to save something now. Save the trees, save the bees, save the whales, save the snails. And the supreme arrogance? Save the planet! Are these people kidding? Save the planet? We don't even know how to take care of ourselves; we haven't learned how to care for one another. We're gonna save the fuckin' planet?

Greens Eat Shit

I'm gettin' tired of that shit. I'm tired of fuckin' Earth Day. I'm tired of these self-righteous environmentalist, white, bourgeois liberals who think the only thing wrong with this country is that there aren't enough bike paths. Tryin' to make the world safe for their repulsive Volvos.

Besides, environmentalists don't give a shit about the planet anyway. Not really. Not in the abstract. You know what they're interested in? A clean place to live. Their own habitat. That's all. They're worried that sometime in the future they might personally be inconvenienced. Narrow, unenlightened self-interest doesn't impress me.

And, by the way, there's nothing wrong with the planet in the first place. The planet is fine. The people are fucked! Compared with the people, the planet is doin' great. It's been here over four billion years. Did you ever think about that? The planet has been here four and a half billion years. And we've been here for what? A hundred thousand? And we've only been engaged in heavy industry for a little over two hundred years. Two hundred versus 4.5 billion! And we have the nerve, the conceit to think that somehow we're a threat? That somehow we're going to put this beautiful little blue-green ball in jeopardy?

Believe me, this planet has put up with much worse than us. It's been through earthquakes, volcanoes, plate tectonics, solar flares, sunspots, magnetic storms, pole reversals, planetary floods, worldwide fires, tidal waves, wind and water erosion, cosmic rays, ice ages, and hundreds of thousands of years of bombardment by comets, asteroids, and meteors. And people think a few plastic bags and aluminum cans are going to make a difference?

See Ya!

The planet isn't goin' anywhere, folks. We are! We're goin' away. Pack your shit, we're goin' away. And we won't leave much of a trace. Thank God for that. Nothing left. Maybe a little Styrofoam. The planet will be here, and we'll be gone. Another failed mutation; another closed-end biological mistake.

The planet will shake us off like a bad case of fleas. And it will heal itself, because that's what the planet does; it's a self-correcting system. The air and water and earth will recover and be renewed. And if plastic is really not degradable, well, most likely the planet will incorporate it into a new paradigm: The Earth Plus Plastic. Earth doesn't share our prejudice against plastic. Plastic came out of the earth. She probably sees it as one of her many children.

In fact, it could be the reason the earth allowed us to be spawned in the first place; it wanted plastic and didn't know how to make it. It needed us. That could be the answer to our age-old question: "Why are we here?" "Plastic, assholes!"

"I Just Can't Shake This Cold"

And so, our job is done. The plastic is here, we can now be phased out. And I think that's already begun, don't you? I mean, to be fair, the planet probably sees us as a mild threat, something to be dealt with. And I'm sure it can defend itself in the manner of a large organism; the way a beehive or an ant colony would muster a defense. I'm sure the planet will think of something. What would you be thinking if you were the planet, trying to defend yourself against this pesky, troublesome species?

"Let's see, what might I try? Hmmm! Viruses might be good; these humans seem vulnerable. And viruses are tricky, always mutating and developing new strains when new medicines or vaccines are introduced. And perhaps the first virus I try could be one that compromises their immune systems. A human immunodeficiency virus that makes them vulnerable to other infections that come along. And perhaps this virus could be spread sexually, making them reluctant to engage in the act of reproduction, further reducing their numbers."

Well, I guess it's a poetic notion, but it's a start. And I can dream, can't I?

No, folks, I don't worry about the little things. Bees, trees, whales, snails. I don't worry about them. I think we're part of a much greater wisdom. Greater than we will ever understand. A higher order. Call it what you like. I call it The Big Electron. The Big Electron. It doesn't punish, it doesn't reward, and it doesn't judge. It just is. And so are we. For a little while. See ya.

WHAT'S MY MOTIVATION?

What's all this stuff about motivation? I say, if you need motivation, you probably need more than motivation. You probably need chemical intervention or brain surgery. Actually, if you ask me, this country could do with a little *less* motivation. The people who are causing all the trouble seem highly motivated to me. Serial killers, stock swindlers, drug dealers, Christian Republicans. I'm not sure motivation is always a good thing. You show me a lazy prick who's lying in bed all day, watching TV, only occasionally getting up to piss, and I'll show you a guy who's not causing any trouble.

THE "PRE-" EPIDEMIC

Preboard, prescreen, prerecord, pretaped, preexisting, preorder, preheat, preplan, pretest, precondition, preregister. In nearly all of these cases you can drop the "pre" and not change the meaning of the word.

"The suicide film was not prescreened by the school." No, of course not. It was screened.

"You can call and prequalify for a loan over the phone. Your loan is preapproved." Well, if my loan is approved before I call then no approval is necessary. The loan is simply available.

NAME IT LIKE IT IS

The words *Fire Department* make it sound like they're the ones who are starting the fires, doesn't it? It should be called the "Extinguishing Department." We don't call the police the "Crime Department." Also, the "Bomb Squad" sounds like a terrorist gang. The same is true of *wrinkle cream*. Doesn't it sound like it causes wrinkles? And why would a doctor prescribe pain pills? I already *have* pain! I need relief pills!

KEEP IT—WE DON'T WANT IT

Don't you get tired of celebrities who explain their charity work by saying they feel they have to "give something back." I don't feel that way. I didn't take nothin'. You can search my house; I didn't take a thing. Everything I got, I worked for, and it was given to me freely. I also paid taxes on it. Late! I paid late. But I paid. You celebrity people wanna give something back? How about giving back half the money? Or a couple of those houses? And you dickwads who collect cars? How about giving back 50 or 60 of them? Or maybe, if you people really want to give something back, you could let go of a little of that arrogance.

PEOPLE I CAN DO WITHOUT
(PART 1)

- A stranger on the train who wants to tell me about his bowel movements.
- People who whistle cowboy songs during a funeral.
- Anyone who refers to Charles Manson as "Chuck."
- A tall man with a Slavic accent wearing a bow tie of human flesh.
- Any couple who owns "his and hers" rectal thermometers.
- A girl whose wallet contains nude photos of Sam Donaldson or Yasser Arafat.
- A man with a tattoo that shows Joey Buttafuoco dancing the Lambada with Leona Helmsley.
- Any man who can ingest a quart of vegetable soup through his nose in one long suck.
- A priest with an eye patch and a limp who's selling pieces of the cross.
- Any guy named Dogmeat whose body has over six square feet of scar tissue.
- Anyone who takes off work on Ted Bundy's birthday.
- A man with gold front teeth who wants to play stud poker on the floor of the bus station men's room.

- A crying woman with a harpoon gun entering a sports bar.
- Anyone who gets plastic surgery in an attempt to look more intelligent.
- A man with one cloven hoof who wants to give my daughter a hysterectomy.
- A seventy-year-old man wearing gag underpants that say "We visited the Grassy Knoll."
- Any man with a birthmark shaped like a hypodermic needle.
- Any woman who repeatedly gives me a high five during sex.
- A cross-eyed man in a New Year's hat reciting "Casey at the Bat" in Latin.
- Anyone who receives e-mail from Willard Scott.
- A man who plunges a bone-handled carving fork through his neck in order to get my attention.
- Anyone with three nostrils.
- A bag lady wearing over 200 garments, including nine separate hats.
- Any man who tries to pierce his ear with an electric can opener.
- A retarded twelve-year-old who carries more than six books of matches.
- Any man who gives himself a Harvey Wallbanger enema. On the rocks.
- Any person bleeding from three orifices who wants me to cosign on a loan.
- A homely, flat-chested woman wearing a Foxy Lady T-shirt.

EXPRESSIONS I QUESTION
(PART I)

IN THE PRIVACY OF YOUR OWN HOME. As opposed to what? The privacy of someone else's home? You have no privacy in someone else's home; that's why you got your own home.

DOWN THE PIKE. "He was the meanest guy ever to come down the pike." Fine. What about guys who come *up* the pike? Not everyone lives "north of the pike." Some guys have to come *up* the pike, and they're really mean, because nobody mentions them at all. And what about a guy who doesn't even *use* the pike? He arrives on Amtrak! "Boy, he was the meanest guy ever to arrive on Amtrak." Doesn't sound right.

LIKE A BAT OUT OF HELL. We say some guy was "goin' like a bat outta Hell." How do we know how fast a bat would leave Hell? Maybe he would leave real slow. In fact, why should we assume that a bat would even want to leave Hell? Maybe he likes it there. Maybe Hell is just right for a bat. Maybe it's bat heaven. And now that we're on this subject, how do we know Hell has bats in the first place? What would a bat be doin' in Hell? Usually a bat is in the belfry. Why would he want to split his time between two places? Then again, maybe that's why he's in such a hurry to leave Hell. He's due back at the belfry.

Why do we say **OUT LIKE A LIGHT?** The primary function of a light is to be lit, not to be out. Why choose a light to represent the concept of being out? Why not, "*On* like a light?" The same is true of **DROPPING LIKE FLIES;** the wrong quality is being emphasized. Flies are known for flying, not dropping. And let's forget **METEORIC RISE.** Meteors don't rise, they fall.

YOU CAN TALK UNTIL YOU'RE BLUE IN THE FACE, ETC. ETC. Well, you can't talk until you're blue in the face. In order to talk, you need oxygen. Blueness of the face is caused by a lack of oxygen. So, if you're blue in the face, you probably stopped talking a long time ago. You might be making some gestures. In fact, if you're running out of oxygen, I would imagine you're making quite a number of gestures. And rather flamboyant ones at that.

When we point out someone's lack of popularity, especially a politician's, we sometimes say, **HE COULDN'T GET ELECTED DOG CATCHER.** First of all, since when do they elect dog catchers? I've never seen one on the ballot, have you? The last time you were in the voting booth, did it say, "President, Vice President, Dog Catcher?" No. And why do they imply that getting elected dog catcher would be easy? I think it would be hard. A lot of people have dogs; they wouldn't vote for you. And many of the people who don't have dogs still like them. I should think it would be quite difficult to get elected dog catcher.

ONE THING LEADS TO ANOTHER. Not always. Sometimes one thing leads to the same thing. Ask an addict.

THE PEN IS MIGHTIER THAN THE SWORD needs to be updated. It's overdue. It should have been changed much earlier in the twentieth century to, "The typewriter is mightier than the machine gun." But at this point it should probably read, "The word processor is mightier than the particle-beam weapon."

UNIDENTIFIED PERSON. What exactly is an "unidentified person"? Doesn't everyone have an identity? Maybe they mean he's a person they can't identify. But that would make him an "unidentifiable person." I guess if nothing else, he could always be referred to as "that guy we can't identify."

OPEN A CAN OF WORMS. Why would you have to open it? Are there really sealed cans of worms? Who sealed them? Worms are usually put in a can *after* it has been opened, and emptied of something else, like corn or pumpkin meat. Uncover a can of worms, maybe. But not *open.*

WILD AND WOOLLY. Whenever I hear something described as wild and woolly, I always wonder where the woolly part comes in. Wild I understand. But woolly? I have some sweaters that are woolly, but they're kind of conservative. Not wild at all.

IN THE WRONG PLACE AT THE WRONG TIME. How can this be? Shouldn't it be, "In the *right* place at the wrong time?" If a guy gets hit by a stray bullet, he is in the right place (where his day's activities have taken him) at the wrong time (when a bullet is passing by). If it were the wrong place, the bullet wouldn't have been there.

IN THE RIGHT PLACE AT THE RIGHT TIME is also questionable. Let's say a guy wins a prize for being a bank's millionth customer. All you really have to say is, "He was in the right place." After all, it *had* to be the right time. That's the only time they were giving away the prize. If it hadn't been the right time, it wouldn't have been the right place. Twenty minutes later the bank wouldn't be "the right place" anymore.

YOU NEVER KNOW. Not true. Sometimes you know.

YOU DON'T HAVE TO BE A ROCKET SCIENTIST implies that rocket scientists are somehow smart. How smart can they be? They build machines that travel thousands of miles to drop fire and radiation on people. That doesn't sound smart to me.

THE OLDEST TRICK IN THE BOOK. Sometimes in the movies, when the bad guy is holding a gun on the good guy, the good guy says, "It won't work, Scarfelli. My men are right behind you with their guns drawn." And the bad guy says, "You can't fool me, Murdoch, that's the oldest trick in the book." Well, exactly what book are these guys talking about? Have you ever seen a book with a bunch of tricks in it? Magic tricks maybe, but I don't think the thing with the guns would be in there, do you? A prostitute might have a book of tricks, but once again, probably no mention of the two guys with the guns. And anyway, even if there really were a book with a lot of tricks in it, how would you know which trick was the oldest? They were all printed at the same time. You'd have to say, "You can't fool me, Murdoch, that's the trick that appears earliest in the book." But that's not good movie dialogue, is it?

When they say someone is **NOT GOING TO WIN ANY POPULARITY CONTESTS,** what popularity contests are they talking about? I've never heard of these contests. Where do they have them? And who wins? Whoever is winning these popularity contests can't be that popular. You never hear about them.

YOU COULD HEAR A PIN DROP. Well, you can't hear a pin drop. Not even a bowling pin. When a pin is dropping, it's just floating through the air. There's very little noise. You might be able to hear a pin land but certainly not drop.

SOME FAVORITE EUPHEMISMS

[all euphemisms actually observed]

blow job = holistic massage therapy

cheap hotel = limited service lodging

loan-sharking = interim financing

kidnapping = custodial interference

mattress and box spring = sleep system

shack job = live-in companion

truck stop = travel plaza

used videocassette = previously viewed cassette

manicurist = nail technician

nude beach = clothing optional beach

peephole = observation port

baldness = acquired uncombable hair

body bags = remains pouches

drought = deficit water situation

recession = a meaningful downturn in aggregate output

in love = emotionally involved

room clerk = guest service agent

MORE FAVORITE EUPHEMISMS

uniforms = career apparel

seat belt/air bag = impact management system

dildo = marital aid

nonbelievers = the unchurched

lying on a job application = résumé enhancement

miscarriage = pregnancy loss

police clubs = batons

smuggling = commodity relocation

porn star = adult entertainer

nightclub = party space

monkey bars = pipe-frame exercise unit

cardboard box = makeshift home

fingerprinting = digital imaging

fat lady = big woman

junkies = the user population

apartment = dwelling unit

committee = task force

maid = room attendant

salesman = product specialist

EVEN MORE
FAVORITE EUPHEMISMS

bad loans = nonperforming assets

seasickness = motion discomfort

gangs = nontraditional organized crime

civilian deaths = collateral damage

mole = beauty mark

garbage collection = environmental services

breast = white meat

thigh = dark meat

sludge = bio-solids

genocide = ethnic cleansing

Jeep = sports utility vehicle

library = learning resources center

junk mail = direct marketing

soda jerk = fountain attendant

soldiers and weapons = military assets

third floor = level three

illegal immigrant = guest worker

Jet ski = personal watercraft

loafers = slip-ons

GET A LIFE

One morning I get up, get out of bed, get showered, get some breakfast, and get to thinkin', "I'm not gettin' any." I get the urge to get some nookie, and get an idea. So I get dressed, get in my car, and get on the freeway.

When I get downtown, I get a few beers, get a buzz, and get lucky. I get a glimpse of a fine-looking woman. I get her a drink, get her talking, and we get acquainted. So I get up my courage and get her to agree to go get a room.

We get outta there, get some booze, get in a taxi, and get a hotel.

We get in the room, and get comfortable, and I'm gettin' excited 'cause I'm gonna get in her pants. So we get undressed, get in bed, and get started. And I'm gettin' hot 'cause she's gettin' horny. She wants to get down, and I wanna get my rocks off. I wanna get it up, get in, get it on, get off, and get out.

And it starts gettin' real good. But then I get thinking, "Suppose I get the clap? If I get the clap, I'll have to get shots. Might get worse. Could get AIDS. Shoulda got rubbers."

Now I get paranoid. Get a bit crazy. Get a bit scared.

Gotta get a grip.

Then it gets worse. Suppose she gets pregnant? Will she get an abortion? She might wanna get married. I can't get involved.

If I gotta get married, I gotta get her a ring. How do I get it? I'd have to get credit. Or get hold of some money!

That means gettin' a job. Or gettin' a gun. And a getaway car. But suppose I get caught? Get busted by cops. Get thrown in the jail! Gotta get help. Get a good lawyer. Get out on bail.

No. I gotta get serious. Get it together. Get with the program. Get me a break, get me a job. Get a promotion, get a nice raise, get a new house, and get some respect. But if I get all of that, I can't get real cocky. Might get someone mad who'd get on my case, get me in trouble, and then I'd get fired.

Then I'd get mad, maybe get violent, get kicked outta work. Then get discouraged, start to get desperate, get hold of some drugs, get loaded, get hooked, and get sick. Get behind in my rent, get evicted, get thrown on the street.

Maybe get mugged, get beaten, get injured, get hospitalized, get operated on, get a blood clot, get a heart attack, get the last rites, get a stroke, get a flat line, get a trip to the graveyard, and get buried in a field.

So get this. You gotta get smart, and you gotta get real. Get serious. Get home, get undressed, get in bed, get some sleep. Or you might just get fucked. Get me?

MARRY AN ORPHAN

Men, take my advice, marry an orphan. It's great. First of all, there are never any in-law problems. Second, there are no annoying Thanksgiving and Christmas visits sitting around pretending to enjoy the company of a couple of fifth-generation nitwits. In fact, when it comes to visiting her folks, the worst thing that might happen to you would be an occasional trip to the cemetery to leave some cheap flowers. And you might even get out of that by claiming a morbid fear of headstones.

But most important, as the relationship is just beginning, you won't have to worry about making a good impression on the girl's parents, nor will you have to get her father's approval. Believe me when I tell you, when you say, "I hope your father will approve of me," there is no greater thrill than having your beloved turn to you brightly and say, "My father's dead."

I'VE GOT YOUR SANCTITY OF LIFE

One phrase that comes up quite a bit in abortion discussions is "sanctity of life." What about that? Do you think there's such a thing as sanctity of life? Personally, I think it's a bunch of shit. Who says life is sacred? God? Great, but if you read your history you know that God is one of the leading causes of death and has been for thousands of years. Hindus, Moslems, Christians, Jews, all taking turns killing one another, because God told them it was a good idea. The sword of God, the blood of the lamb, vengeance is mine. Millions of dead people. All because they gave the wrong answer to the God Question:

"Do you believe in God?"

"No."

BAM! Dead.

"How about you? Do you believe in God?"

"Yes."

"Do you believe in *my* God?"

"No."

BAM! Dead!

"My god has a bigger dick than your god."

For thousands of years all the bloodiest and most brutal wars have been based on religious hatred. Which, of course, is fine with me; any time "holy" people are killing one another, I'm a happy guy. But please, don't kill each other and then give me that shit about "sanctity of life." Even if there were such an absurd thing, I don't think you could blame it on God.

You know where the sanctity of life comes from? We made it up. You know why? Because we're alive. Self-interest! Living people have a strong incentive to promote the idea that somehow life is sacred. You don't see Bing Crosby runnin' around talking about this shit, do you? You don't hear much from Mussolini on the subject. And what's the latest from JFK? Not a goddamn thing! You know why? Because JFK, Mussolini, and Bing Crosby are all fuckin' dead. They're fuckin' dead, and dead people give less than a shit about the sanctity of life.

The only people who care about it are the living. So the whole thing grows out of a biased point of view. It's a self-serving, man-made bullshit story; one of those things we tell ourselves in order to feel noble. "Life is sacred." Makes us feel good. But let me ask you this: If everything that ever lived is dead, and everything alive is going to die, where does the sacred part come in? Can you help me on that?

Because even with all we preach about the sanctity of life, we don't practice it. Look at what we kill: Mosquitoes and flies, because they're pests. Lions and tigers, because it's fun. Chickens and pigs, because we're hungry. And people. We kill people. Because they're pests. And because it's fun!

And here's something else I noticed. Apparently, the sanctity of life doesn't apply to cancer cells, does it? You rarely see a bumper sticker that says Save the Tumors. Or I Brake for Advanced Melanoma. No. Viruses, molds, mildew, maggots, fungus, weeds, intestinal worms, *E. coli* bacteria, the crabs. Nothin' sacred about those things. Just us.

So, at best, the sanctity of life is a selective thing. We choose which forms of life we feel are sacred, and we get to kill the rest. Pretty neat deal. You know how we got it? We made the whole thing up! Same way we made up the death penalty. The sanctity of life, and the death penalty. We're such a versatile species.

YOUR CHILDREN ARE OVERRATED

Something else I'm getting tired of in this country is all this stupid bullshit I have to listen to about children. That's all you hear anymore, children: "Help the children, save the children, protect the children." You know what I say? Fuck the children! Fuck 'em! Fuck kids; they're getting entirely too much attention.

And I know what some of you are thinking: "Jesus, he's not going to attack children, is he?" Yes he is! He's going to attack children. And remember, this is Mr. Conductor talking; I know what I'm talking about.

And I also know that all you boring single dads and working moms, who think you're such fuckin' heroes, aren't gonna like this, but somebody's gotta tell you for your own good: your children are overrated and overvalued, and you've turned them into little cult objects. You have a child fetish, and it's not healthy. And don't give me all that weak shit, "Well, I love my children." Fuck you! Everybody loves their children; it doesn't make you special.

John Wayne Gacy loved his children. Yes, he did. He kept 'em all right out in the yard, near the garage. That's not what I'm talking about. What I'm talking about is this constant, mindless yammering in the media, this neurotic fixation that suggests somehow everything—*everything*—has to revolve around the lives of children. It's completely out of balance.

Let's Get Real

Listen, there are a couple of things about kids you have to remember. First of all, they're not all cute. In fact, if you look at 'em real close, most of them are rather unpleasant looking. And a lot of them don't smell too good either. The little ones in particular seem to have a kind of urine and sour-milk combination that I don't care for at all. Stay with me on this, folks, the sooner you face it the better off you're gonna be.

Second premise: not all children are smart and clever. Got that? Kids are like any other group of people: a few winners, a whole lot of losers! This country is *filled* with loser kids who simply . . . aren't . . . going anywhere! And there's nothing you can do about it, folks. Nothing! You can't save 'em all. You can't do it. You gotta let 'em go; you gotta cut 'em loose; you gotta stop overprotecting them, because you're making 'em too soft. Today's kids are way too soft.

Safe *and* Sorry

For one thing, there's too much emphasis on safety and safety equipment: childproof medicine bottles, fireproof pajamas, child restraints, car seats. And helmets! Bicycle, baseball, skateboard, scooter helmets. Kids have to wear helmets now for everything but jerking off. Grown-ups have taken all the fun out of being a kid, just to save a few thousand lives. It's pathetic.

What's happened is, these baby boomers, these soft, fruity baby boomers, have raised an entire generation of soft, fruity kids who aren't even allowed to have hazardous toys, for Chrissakes! Hazardous toys, shit! Whatever happened to natural selection? Survival of the fittest? The kid who swallows too many marbles doesn't grow up to have kids of his own. Simple stuff. Nature knows best!

We're saving entirely too many lives in this country—of *all* ages! Nature should be permitted to do its job weeding out and killing off the weak and sickly and ignorant people, without interference from airbags and batting helmets. We're lowering the human gene pool! If these ideas bother you, just think of them as passive eugenics.

New Math

Here's another example of overprotection for these kids, and you've seen this one on the news. Did you ever notice that every time some guy with an AK-47 strolls into the school yard and kills three or four of these fuckin' kids and a couple of teachers, the next day the school is overrun with psychologists and psychiatrists and grief counselors and trauma therapists, trying to help the children cope?

Shit! When I was a kid, and some guy came to our school and killed three or four of us, we went right on with our arithmetic: "Thirty-five classmates minus four equals thirty-one." We were tough! I say if a kid can handle the violence at home, he oughta be able to handle the violence at school.

Out of Uniform

Another bunch of ignorant bullshit about your children: school uniforms. Bad theory! The idea that if kids wear uniforms to school, it helps keep order. Hey! Don't these schools do enough damage makin' all these children *think* alike? Now they're gonna get 'em to *look* alike, too?

And it's not even a new idea; I first saw it in old news-reels from the 1930s, but it was hard to understand, because the narration was in German! But the uniforms looked beauti-ful. And the children did everything they were told and never questioned authority. Gee, I wonder why someone would want to put our children in uniforms. Can't imagine.

And one more item about children: this superstitious nonsense of blaming tobacco companies for kids who smoke. Listen! Kids don't smoke because a camel in sunglasses tells them to. They smoke for the same reasons adults do, because it's an enjoyable activity that relieves anxiety and depression.

And you'd be anxious and depressed too if you had to put up with pathetic, insecure, yuppie parents who enroll you in college before you've even figured out which side of the playpen smells the worst and then fill you full of Ritalin to get you in a mood *they* approve of, and drag you all over town in search of empty, meaningless structure: Little League, Cub Scouts, swimming, soccer, karate, piano, bagpipes, watercolors, witchcraft, glass blowing, and dildo practice. It's absurd.

They even have "play dates," for Christ's sake! Playing is now done by appointment! Whatever happened to "You show me your wee-wee, and I'll show you mine"? You never hear that anymore.

But it's true. A lot of these striving, anal parents are burning their kids out on structure. I think what every child needs and ought to have every day is two hours of daydreaming. Plain old daydreaming. Turn off the Internet, the CD-ROMs, and the computer games and let them stare at a tree for a couple of hours. It's good for them. And you know something? Every now and then they actually come up with one of their own ideas. You want to know how you can help your kids? Leave them the fuck alone!

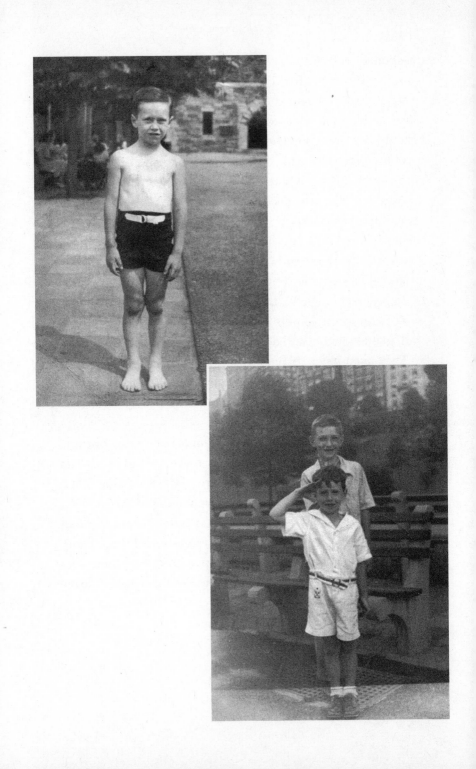

PARENTAL GUIDANCE

What is all this nonsense about parental guidance, parental control, and parental advisories? The whole reason people in this country are as fucked up as they are and make such ignorant decisions on public policy is that they listened too closely to their parents in the first place. This is an authoritarian country with too many laws, rules, controls, and restrictions. "Do this! Don't do that! Shut up! Sit still! No talking! Stand up straight!" No wonder kids are so fucked up; traditional authoritarian values. It starts in kindergarten: They give you a coloring book and some crayons, and tell you, "Be creative . . . but don't go outside the lines." Fuck parents!

FIVE UNEASY MOMENTS

Moment #1

Have you ever been in one of those serious social situations when you suddenly realize you have to pull the underwear out of the crack in your ass?

"Do you, Enrique, take this woman, Blanca, to be your lawful, wedded wife?"

"Huh? Hold on, Rev." [Tugging violently at his pants] "Aah! Got it! Jesus, that was in deep. Yes. Yes, I do. Excuse me, Rev, sometimes my shorts get sucked up way inside my asshole." Ain't love grand?

Moment #2

Have you ever been at a really loud party where the music is deafening, and in order to be heard you have to scream at the top of your lungs? Even if you're talking to the person right next to you? But then often, the music stops suddenly and everyone quiets down at the same time. And only your voice can be heard, ringing across the room:

"CHARLIE, I'M GONNA GET MY TESTICLES LAMINATED!!"

And everyone turns to look at Charlie's interesting friend.

Moment #3

Have you ever been talking to a bunch of guys, and you laugh through your nose and blow a snot on your shirt? And then you have to just keep talking and hope they'll think it's part of the design? It works all right if you're wearing a Hawaiian shirt. But otherwise, they're gonna notice.

"Hey, Ed, check it out! Dave's got a big snot on his shirt! Howie, look! Phil, c'mere! Dave just blew a big snot all over himself."

Guys are such fun.

Moment #4

Did you ever meet a guy, and as you're shaking his hand you realize he doesn't have a complete hand? It feels like something is missing? And you're standing there holding a handful of deformed, knoblike flesh?

It's unnerving, isn't it? But you can't react; you can't even look down at his hand. You have to make believe it feels great.

You can't go, "Eeeaauuu! How creepy! Where's your other fingers?"

You can't say that. It's not even an option. You have to hang in, smile big, and say, "Hey, swell hand! Gimme three! Okay! A high-three! Yo! Okay!"

Moment #5

Have you ever been talking to yourself when someone suddenly comes in the room? And you have to make believe you were singing? And you hope to God the other person really believes there's a song called "Fuck Her"?

EUPHEMISTIC BULLSHIT

I don't like euphemistic language, words that shade the truth. American English is packed with euphemism, because Americans have trouble dealing with reality, and in order to shield themselves from it they use soft language. And somehow it gets worse with every generation.

Here's an example. There's a condition in combat that occurs when a soldier is completely stressed out and is on the verge of nervous collapse. In World War I it was called "shell shock." Simple, honest, direct language. Two syllables. Shell shock. It almost sounds like the guns themselves. That was more than eighty years ago.

Then a generation passed, and in World War II the same combat condition was called "battle fatigue." Four syllables now; takes a little longer to say. Doesn't seem to hurt as much. "Fatigue" is a nicer word than "shock." Shell shock! Battle fatigue.

By the early 1950s, the Korean War had come along, and the very same condition was being called "operational exhaustion." The phrase was up to eight syllables now, and any last traces of humanity had been completely squeezed out of it. It was absolutely sterile: operational exhaustion. Like something that might happen to your car.

Then, barely fifteen years later, we got into Vietnam, and, thanks to the deceptions surrounding that war, it's no surprise that the very same condition was referred to as "post-traumatic stress disorder." Still eight syllables, but we've added a hyphen, and the pain is completely buried under jargon: post-traumatic stress disorder. I'll bet if they had still been calling it "shell shock," some of those Vietnam veterans might have received the attention they needed.

But it didn't happen, and one of the reasons is that soft language; the language that takes the life out of life. And somehow it keeps getting worse.

Here are some more examples. At some point in my life, the following changes occurred:

toilet paper = *bathroom tissue*

sneakers = *running shoes*

false teeth = *dental appliances*

medicine = *medication*

information = *directory assistance*

the dump = *the landfill*

motels = *motor lodges*

house trailers = *mobile homes*

used cars = *previously owned vehicles*

room service = *guest room dining*

riot = *civil disorder*

strike = *job action*

zoo = *wildlife park*

jungle = *rain forest*

swamp = *wetlands*

glasses = *prescription eyewear*

garage = *parking structure*

drug addiction = *substance abuse*

soap opera = *daytime drama*

gambling joint = *gaming resort*

prostitute = *sex worker*

theater = *performing arts center*

wife beating = *domestic violence*

constipation = *occasional irregularity*

Health

When I was a little boy, if I got sick I went to a doctor, who sent me to a hospital to be treated by other doctors. Now I go to a "family practitioner," who belongs to a "health maintenance organization," which sends me to a "wellness center" to be treated by "health-care delivery professionals."

Poverty

Poor people used to live in slums. Now "the economically disadvantaged" occupy "substandard housing" in the "inner cities." And a lot of them are broke. They don't have "negative cash flow." They're broke! Because many of them were fired. In other words, management wanted to "curtail redundancies in the human resources area," and so, many workers are no longer "viable members of the workforce." Smug, greedy, well-fed white people have invented a language to conceal their sins. It's as simple as that.

Government

The CIA doesn't kill anybody, they "neutralize" people. Or they "depopulate" an area. The government doesn't lie, it engages in "disinformation." The Pentagon actually measures nuclear radiation in something called "sunshine units." Israeli murderers are called "commandos," Arab commandos are called "terrorists." The Contra killers were known as "freedom fighters." Well, if crime fighters fight crime and firefighters fight fire, what do freedom fighters fight?

Physical Disorders

And some of this softened language is just silly and embarrassing. On the airlines they say they're going to preboard "passengers in need of special assistance." Cripples. Simple, honest, direct language. There's no shame attached to the word "cripple." No shame. It's a word used in Bible translations: "Jesus healed the cripples." It doesn't take six words to describe that condition.

But we don't have cripples anymore; instead we have the "physically challenged." Is that a grotesque enough evasion for you? How about "differently abled?" I've actually heard cripples referred to as differently abled. You can't even call them handicapped anymore. They say, "We're not handicapped, we're handi-capable." These poor suckers have been bullshitted by the system into believing that if you change the name of the condition, somehow you'll change the condition. Well, it doesn't happen that way.

I'm sure you've noticed we have no deaf people in this country. "Hearing impaired." And no one's blind. "Partially sighted" or "visually impaired." And thank God we no longer have stupid children. Today's kids all have "learning disabilities." Or they're "minimally exceptional." How would you like to be told that about your child? Actually, it sounds faintly positive.

"He's minimally exceptional."

"Oh, thank God for that, I guess."

Best of all, psychologists now call ugly people "those with severe appearance deficits." Things are so bad that any day I expect to hear a rape victim referred to as an unwilling sperm recipient.

Gettin' Old

Of course, it's been obvious for some time that there are no old people in this country. They all died, and what we have are "senior citizens." How's that for a lifeless, typically American, twentieth-century phrase? There's no pulse in a "senior citizen."

But that's a term I've come to accept. That's what old people are going to be called. But the phrase I will continue to resist is when they describe an old person as being "ninety years young." Imagine how sad the fear of aging that is revealed in that phrase. To be unable even to use the word "old"; to have to use its antonym.

And I understand the fear of aging is natural; it's universal, isn't it? No one wants to get old, no one wants to die. But we do. We die. And we don't like that, so we bullshit ourselves.

I started bullshitting myself when I reached my forties. I'd look in the mirror, and say, "Well, I guess I'm getting . . . 'older!'" Older sounds better than old, doesn't it? Sounds like it might even last a little longer. Bullshit. I'm getting old. And it's okay. But the Baby Boomers can't handle that, and remember, the boomers invented most of this soft language. So now they've come up with a new life phase: "pre-elderly." How sad. How relentlessly sad.

Gettin' Dead

But it's all right, folks, because thanks to our fear of death, no one has to die; they can all just pass away. Or expire, like a magazine subscription. If it happens in the hospital, it will be called a terminal episode. The insurance company will refer to it as negative patient-care outcome. And if it's the result of malpractice, they'll say it was a therapeutic misadventure.

To be honest, some of this language makes me want to vomit. Well, perhaps "vomit" is too strong a word. It makes me want to engage in an involuntary, personal protein spill.

INTERVIEW WITH JESUS

Interviewer:
Ladies and Gentlemen, we're privileged to have with us a man known around the world as the Prince of Peace, Jesus Christ.

Jesus:
That's me.

I: *How are you, Jesus?*

J: Fine, thanks, and let me say it's great to be back.

I: *Why, after all this time, have you come back?*

J: Mostly nostalgia.

I: *Can you tell us a little bit about the first time you were here?*

J: Well, there's not much to tell. I think everybody knows the story by now. I was born on Christmas. And actually, that always bothered me, because I only got one present. You know, if I was born a couple of months earlier I would've got two presents. But look, I'm not complaining. After all, it's only material goods.

I: *There's a story that there were three wise men.*

J: Well, there were three kings who showed up. I don't know how wise they were. They didn't *look* very wise. They said they followed a star. That don't sound wise to me.

I: *Didn't they bring gifts?*

J: Yes. Gold, frankincense, and I believe, myrrh, which I never did find out what that was. You don't happen to know what myrrh is, do you?

I: *Well, I believe it's a reddish-brown, bitter gum resin.*

J: Oh, great. Just what I need. What am I gonna do with a gum resin? I'd rather have the money, that way I could buy something I need. You know, something I wouldn't normally buy for myself.

I: *What would that be?*

J: Oh, I don't know. A bathing suit. I never had a bathing suit. Maybe a Devo hat. Possibly a bicycle. I really coulda used a bicycle. Do you realize all the walking I did? I must've crossed Canaan six, eight times. Up and down, north and south, walking and talking, doin' miracles, tellin' stories.

I: *Tell us about the miracles. How many miracles did you perform?*

J: Well, leaving out the loaves and the fishes, a total of 107 miracles.

I: *Why not the loaves and the fishes?*

J: Well, technically that one wasn't a miracle.

I: *It wasn't?*

J: No, it turns out a lot of people were putting them back. They were several days old. And besides, not all those miracles were pure miracles anyway.

I: *What do you mean? If they weren't miracles, what were they?*

J: Well, some of them were parlor tricks, optical illusions, mass hypnosis. Sometimes people were hallucinatin'. I even used acupressure. That's how I cured most of the blind people, acupressure.

I: *So not all of the New Testament is true.*

J: Naaah. Some of the gospel stuff never happened at all. It was just made up. Luke and Mark used a lot of drugs. Luke was a physician, and he had access to drugs. Matthew and John were okay, but Luke and Mark would write anything.

I: *What about raising Lazarus from the dead?*

J: First of all, he wasn't dead, he was hungover. I've told people that.

I: *But in the Bible you said he was dead.*

J: No! I said he *looked* dead. I said, "Jeez, Peter, this guy looks dead!" You see, Lazarus was a very heavy sleeper, plus the day before we had been to a wedding feast, and he had put away a lot of wine.

I: *Ahhh! Was that the wedding feast at Cana, where you changed the water into wine?*

J: I don't know. We went to an awful lot of wedding feasts in those days.

I: *But did you ever really turn water into wine?*

J: Not that I know of. One time I turned apple juice into milk, but I don't recall the water and wine.

I: *All right, speaking of water, let me ask you about another miracle. What about walking on water? Did that really happen?*

J: Oh yeah, that was one that really happened. You see, the problem was, I could do it, and the other guys couldn't. They were jealous. Peter got so mad at me he had these special shoes made, special big shoes, that if you started out walkin' real fast you could stay on top of the water for a while. Then, of course, after a few yards, badda-boom, down he goes right into the water. He sinks like a rock. That's why I called him Peter. Thou art Peter, and upon this rock I shall build my church.

I: *Well, that brings up the Apostles. What can you tell us about the Apostles?*

J: They smelled like bait, but they were a good bunch of guys. Thirteen of them we had.

I: *Thirteen? The Bible says there were only twelve.*

J: Well, that was according to Luke. I told you about Luke. Actually, we had thirteen. We had Peter, James, John, Andrew, Philip, Bartholomew, Matthew, Thomas, James, that's a different James, Thaddeus. How many is that?

I: *That's ten.*

J: Simon, Judas, and Red.

I: *Red?*

J: Yeah, Red the Apostle.

I: *Red the Apostle doesn't appear in the Bible.*

J: Nah, Red kept pretty much to himself. He never came to any of the weddings. He was a little strange; he thought the Red Sea was named after him.

I: *And what about Judas?*

J: Don't get me started on Judas. A completely unpleasant person, okay?

I: *Well, what about the other Apostles, say for instance, Thomas, was he really a doubter?*

J: Believe me, this guy Thomas, you couldn't tell him nothin'. He was always asking me for ID. Soon as I would see him, he would go, "You got any ID?" To this day he doesn't believe I'm God.

I: *And are you God?*

J: Well, partly. I'm a member of the Trinity.

I: *Yes. In fact, you're writing a book about the Trinity.*

J: That's right, it's called *Three's a Crowd*.

I: *As I understand it, it's nothing more than a thinly veiled attack on the Holy Ghost.*

J: Listen, it's not an attack, okay? It happens I don't get along with the Holy Ghost. So I leave him alone. That's it. What he does is his business.

I: *What's the reason?*

J: Well, first of all, he's a wise guy. Every time he shows up, he appears as somethin' different. One day he's a dove, another day he's a tongue of fire. Always foolin' around. I don't bother with the guy. I don't wanna know about him, I don't wanna see him, I don't wanna talk to him.

I: *Well, let me change the subject. Is there really a place called hell?*

J: Oh yeah, there's a hell, all right. There's also a heck. It's not as severe as hell, but we've got a heck and a hell.

I: *What about purgatory?*

J: No, I don't know about no purgatory. We got heaven, hell, heck, and limbo.

I: *What is limbo like?*

J: I don't know. No one is allowed in. If anyone was in there it wouldn't be limbo, it would just be another place.

I: *Getting back to your previous visit, what can you tell us about the Last Supper?*

J: Well, first of all, if I'da known I was gonna be crucified, I woulda had a bigger meal. You never want to be crucified on an empty stomach. As it was, I had a little salad and some veal.

I: *The crucifixion must have been terrible.*

J: Oh yeah, it was awful. Unless you went through it yourself, you could never know how painful it was. And tiring. It was very, very tiring. But I think more than anything else, it was embarrassing. You know, in front of all those people, to be crucified like that. But, I guess it redeemed a lot of people. I hope so. It would be a shame to do it for no reason.

I: *Were you scared?*

J: Oh yeah. I was afraid it was gonna rain; I thought for sure I would get hit by lightning. One good thing, though, while I was up there I had a really good view; I could actually see my house. There's always a bright side.

I: *And then three days later you rose from the dead.*

J: How's that?

I: *On Easter Sunday. You rose from the dead, didn't you?*

J: Not that I know of. I think I would remember something like that. I do remember sleeping a long time after the crucifixion. Like I said, it was very tiring. I think what mighta happened was I passed out, and they *thought* I was dead. We didn't have such good medical people in those days. It was mostly volunteers.

I: *And, according to the Bible, forty days later you ascended into heaven.*

J: Pulleys! Ropes, pulleys, and a harness. I think it was Simon came up with a great harness thing that went under my toga. You couldn't see it at all. Since that day, I been in Heaven, and, all in all, I would have to say that while I was down here I had a really good time. Except for the suffering.

I: *And what do you think about Christianity today?*

J: Well, I'm a little embarrassed by it. I wish they would take my name off it. If I had the whole thing to do over, I would probably start one of those Eastern religions like Buddha. Buddha was smart. That's how come he's laughing.

I: *You wouldn't want to be a Christian?*

J: No, I wouldn't want to be a member of any group whose symbol is a man nailed onto some wood. Especially if it's me. Buddha's laughing, meanwhile I'm on the cross.

I: *I have a few more questions, do you mind?*

J: Hey, be my guest, how often do I get here?

I: *Are there really angels?*

J: Well, not as many as we used to have. Years ago we had millions of them. Today you can't get the young people to join. It got too dangerous with all the radar and heat-seeking missiles.

I: *What about guardian angels? Are there such things?*

J: Yes, we still have guardian angels, but now, with the population explosion, it's one angel for every six people. Years ago everybody had his own angel.

I: *Do you really answer prayers?*

J: No. First of all, what with sun spots and radio interference, a lot of them don't even get through. And between you and me, we just don't have the staff to handle the workload anymore. In the old days we took pride in answering every single prayer, but like I said, there were less people. And in those days people prayed for something simple, to light a fire, to catch a yak, something like that. But today you got people praying for hockey teams, for longer fingernails, to lose weight. We just can't keep up.

I: *Well, I think we're about out of time. I certainly want to thank you for visiting with us.*

J: Hey, no sweat.

I: *Do you have any words of advice?*

J: You mean like how to remove chewing gum from a suede garment? Something like that?

I: *No, I mean spiritual advice.*

J: Well, I don't know how spiritual it is, but I'd say one thing is don't give your money to the church. They should be giving their money to you.

I: *Well, thank you, Jesus, and good night.*

J: Well, good night, thanks for having me on here today. And by the way, in case anyone is interested, bell-bottoms will be coming back in the year 2015. Ciao.

THE GRIEF/TRAGEDY/SYMPATHY
INDUSTRY

Everyone complains about this being a "victim society." Well, I don't know about the victim society, but I would like to talk about the "Grief, Tragedy, and Sympathy Industry."

The news media are playing a game with you. You're being fed a large ration of other people's troubles designed to keep your mind off the things that should really be bothering you. I guess the media figure if you're sitting around feeling sorry for every sick, injured, or dead person they can scrounge up, you'll have less time to dwell on how fucked up your own life is, and what bad shape this culture is really in.

I'm not so much opposed to grief per se, as I am to public media grief. My attitude is fuck sick people and fuck a dead person. Unless I knew them. And, if so, I'll handle it on my own, thank you. I don't need media guidance to experience sorrow.

Above all, I object to the abuse of the word *tragedy*. Every time some asshole stops breathing these days it's called a tragedy. The word has been devalued. You can't call every death a tragedy and expect the word to mean anything. For instance, multiple deaths do not automatically qualify as tragedies. Just because a man kills his wife and three kids, her lover, his lover, the baby-sitter, the mailman, the Amway lady, and the guy from Publishers Clearing House and then blows his own brains out doesn't mean a tragedy has occurred. It's interesting. It's entertaining to read about. But it's not a tragedy.

The death of a child is also not automatically a tragedy. Some guy backing over his kid in the driveway is not a tragedy, it's a bad, bad mistake. A tragedy is a literary work in which the main character comes to ruin as a consequence of a moral weakness or a fatal flaw. Shakespeare wrote tragedies. A family of nine being wiped out when a train hits their camper is not a tragedy. It's called a traffic accident.

You wanna know what a tragedy is? A tragedy is when you see some fat bastard in the airport with pockmarks on his face and his belly hanging out, and he's with a woman who has bad teeth and multiple bruises, and that night he's gonna make her suck his dick. That's a tragedy. They don't mention that a lot on TV.

The media often refer to the killing of a white policeman as a *tragedy*. Why is that more tragic than the same white policeman killing an unarmed black kid? Why is it never a tragedy on TV when a white cop kills a black kid? It's never presented in that way. The whites save *tragedy* for themselves. Why is that?

The media have elevated the marketing of bathos and sympathy to a fine art. But I gotta tell ya, I really don't care about a paraplegic who climbs a mountain and then skis cross-country for 50 miles; I'm not interested in a one-legged veteran who ice skates across Canada to raise money for children's prosthetics. I have no room for some guy without a nervous system who becomes the state wrestling champion; or a man who loses his torso in Vietnam and later holds his breath for six months to promote spina bifida research; or someone born with no heart who lives to be ninety-five and helps everyone in his neighborhood neaten up their lawns.

Is this all we can find in America that passes for personal drama? People overcoming long odds? God, it's so boring and predictable.

And does this mean we are supposed to admire people simply because of the order of their luck? Because their bad luck came first? What about the reverse? What about people who start well and then fail spectacularly in life? People who were born with every privilege and given every possible gift and talent, who had all the money they needed, were surrounded by good people, and then went out and fucked their lives up anyway? Isn't that drama too? Isn't that equally interesting? In fact, I find it more interesting. More like true tragedy.

I'd prefer to hear something like that once in a while, rather than this pseudo-inspirational bullshit that the media feel they have to feed us in order to keep our minds off America's decline. If they're going to insist that we really need to know about sick babies and cripples who tap dance and quadriplegic softball players, why don't they simply have a special television program called "Inspirational Stories"? That way I can turn the fuckin' thing off. I'm tired of people battling the odds. Fuck the odds. And fuck the people who battle them.

After a while don't you just get weary of being told that some kid in Minnesota needs a new liver? Kids didn't need new livers when I was growing up. We had good livers. What are they feeding these kids that suddenly they all need new livers? I think it's the gene pool. Nature used to eliminate the weak, imperfect kids before they were old enough to reproduce their flaws. Now we have a medical industry dedicated to keeping people alive just long enough to pass along their bad genes to another generation. It's medical arrogance, and it works against nature's plan. I'm sick of hearing about a baby being kept alive on a resuscitator while doctors wait for a kidney to be flown in on a private jet contributed by some corporation seeking good publicity because they just killed six thousand people in Pakistan with a chemical spill. I'm tired of this shit being presented in the context of real news. Prurient gossip about sick people is not real news. It's emotional pandering.

The real news is that there are millions upon millions of sick babies and cripples and addicts and criminals and misfits and diseased and mentally ill and hungry people who need help. Not to mention all the middle-class normals who swear things are just fine but spend three hours a day commuting, and whose dull, meaningless lives are being stolen from them by soulless corporations. But the media don't bother with all that. They like to simply cover their designated Victims of the Week, so they can see themselves as somehow noble. They highlight certain cases, making them appear exceptional. And when they do, they admit they are simply unable and unwilling to report the totality of the Great American Social Nightmare.

GOD HAS GOTTA GO

I make fun of people who are religious, because I think they're fundamentally weak. But I want you to know that on a personal level, when it comes to believing in God, I tried. I really, really tried. I tried to believe there is a God, who created us in his own image, loves us very much, and keeps a close eye on things.

I tried to believe it. But I have to tell you, the longer you live, the more you look around, the more you realize . . . something is fucked. Something is wrong. War, disease, death, destruction, hunger, filth, poverty, torture, crime, corruption, and the Ice Capades. Something is definitely wrong.

If this is the best God can do, I'm not impressed. Results like these do not belong on the résumé of a supreme being. This is the kind of stuff you'd expect from an office temp with a bad attitude. In any well-managed universe, this guy would've been out on his all-powerful ass a long time ago.

So, if there is a God—if there is—I think reasonable people might agree he's at least incompetent and maybe, just maybe, he doesn't give a shit. Which I admire in a person, and which would explain a lot of his results.

I Got the Sun in the Mornin'

So, rather than becoming just another mindless, religious robot, blindly believing that everything is in the hands of some spooky, incompetent father figure who doesn't give a shit, I decided to look around for something else to worship. Something I could really count on. And immediately, I thought of the sun. It happened in an instant. Overnight, I became a sun worshipper.

Well, not overnight; you can't see the sun in the dark. But first thing the next morning, I became a sun worshipper. For several reasons: First of all, I can see the sun. Unlike some other gods I could mention, I can actually see the sun. I'm big on that. If I can see something, it kind of helps the credibility.

Every day I can see the sun as it gives me everything I need: heat, light, food, flowers in the park, reflections on the lake. An occasional skin cancer, but, hey! At least there are no crucifixions. And we sun worshippers don't go around killing other people simply because they don't agree with us.

Sun worship is fairly simple. There's no mystery, no miracles, no pageantry, no one asks for money, there are no songs to learn, and we don't have a special building where we all gather once a week to compare clothing. And the best thing about the sun . . . it never tells me I'm unworthy. It doesn't tell me I'm a bad person who needs to be saved. Hasn't said an unkind word. Treats me fine.

Praying on My Mind

So I worship the sun. But I don't pray to the sun. You know why? Because I wouldn't presume on our friendship. It's not polite. I've often thought people treat God rather rudely.

Trillions and trillions of prayers every day, asking and pleading and begging for favors. "Do this; give me that; I need this; I want that." And most of this praying takes place on Sunday, his day off! It's not nice, and it's no way to treat a friend.

But still people do pray and they pray for many different things. And that's all right with me. I say, pray for anything you want. Pray for anything. But . . . what about the Divine Plan? Remember that? The Divine Plan? A long time ago, God came up with a Divine Plan. He gave it a lot of thought, he decided it was a good plan, and he put it into practice. And for billions and billions of years the Divine Plan has been doing just fine.

But now you come along and pray for something. Well, suppose the thing you're praying for isn't in God's Divine Plan? What do you want him to do? Change his plan? Just for you? Isn't that sort of arrogant? It's a Divine Plan! What good is being God if every rundown schmuck with a two-dollar prayer book can come along and fuck with your plan?

And here's another problem you might encounter. Suppose your prayers aren't answered? What do you do then? What do you say? "Well, it's God's will. Thy will be done"? Fine. But if it's God's will, and he's going to do what he wants anyway, why bother praying in the first place? Doesn't it seem like a big waste of time? Couldn't you just skip the praying part and go straight to "his will"? It's all very confusing to me.

To Each His Own

So, to get around all this, I decided to worship the sun. But as I said, I don't pray to the sun. You know who I pray to? Joe Pesci. Two reasons. First of all, I think he's a pretty good actor. To me, that counts. Second, he looks like a guy who can get things done. Joe doesn't fuck around. In fact, he came through on a couple of things that God was having trouble with. For years I asked God to do something about my noisy neighbor's barking dog. Nothing happened. But Joe Pesci? He straightened that shit out with one visit. It's amazing what you can accomplish with a simple piece of athletic equipment.

So, I've been praying to Joe for a couple of years now, and I've noticed something. I've noticed that all the prayers I used to offer to God and all the prayers I now offer to Joe Pesci are being answered at about the same 50 percent rate. Half the time I get what I want, half the time I don't. Same as God. Fifty-fifty. Same as the four-leaf clover, the horseshoe, the wishing well, and the rabbit's foot. Same as the mojo man, or the voodoo lady who tells you your fortune by squeezing a goat's testicles. It's all the same, fifty-fifty. So just pick a superstition you like, sit back, make a wish, and enjoy yourself.

Tell Me a Story, Daddy

And for those of you who look to the Bible for its moral lessons and literary qualities, I have a couple of other stories I'd like to recommend. You might want to try "The Three Little Pigs." That's a good one, it has a nice happy ending. Then there's "Little Red Riding Hood," although it does have that one X-rated part where the Big Bad Wolf actually eats the grandmother. Which I didn't care for.

And finally, I've always drawn a great deal of moral comfort from Humpty Dumpty. The part I like best: "All the king's horses and all the king's men couldn't put Humpty Dumpty back together again." That's because there is no Humpty Dumpty. And there is no God. None, not one, never was. No God. Sorry.

BULLETS FOR BELIEVERS

I don't worry about guns in school. You know what I'm happy about? Guns in church! This is a terrific development, isn't it? And finally it's here! I'm so happy. I prayed for this. Oddly enough, I actually prayed for this. And I predicted it, too.

A couple of years ago I said that pretty soon there'd be some fuckin' yo-yo Christian with a Bible and a rifle who'd go apeshit in a church and kill six people. And the media would refer to him as a "disgruntled worshiper." I had no idea it would be a non-Christian. That's a really nice touch.

And my hat is off to the people of Texas for once again leading the way when it comes to the taking of human life. Texans are always in the vanguard of this important activity, and here they are again, setting a good example, showing the way. And finally they're going after the right people: the churchgoers. Let's face it, folks. They're askin' for it. They just want to be with Jesus. Give them a helping hand.

"Wanna see the Lord?" BANG! "Off you go!" BANG! "Are you a Christian?" BANG! "Say hello to Jesus!"

Give 'em a Christian helping hand. Don't think they wouldn't do the same for you. They don't call themselves "Christian soldiers" for nothing.

SOME LIKE IT HOT

Think for a moment about flamethrowers. The fact that we have them at all. Well, actually we don't have them, the army has them. You know, I hadn't thought of that; the army has all the flamethrowers. I'd say we're jolly well fucked if we have to go up against the army, wouldn't you?

My point is that there are even such things as flamethrowers in the first place. What it indicates to me is that at some point, some person, Phil perhaps, said to himself, "Look at all those people across the road. What I wouldn't give to set them on fire. But I'm much too far away. If only I had some device that would shoot flames on them."

Well, the whole thing might've ended right there, but Phil happened to mention it to his friend, Dwayne, one of those people who's good with tools. About a month later, Dwayne was back.

"Phil, that idea of yours? Quite a concept. Watch!"

WHOOOOOOSH! WHOOOOOOMPH! CRACKLE! BURN!

Before long, the army came around. "Hi, boys. We want to buy 500,000 of those flamethrowers. We have a long list of people we'd like to set on fire. Give us 500,000 and have them camouflaged. We don't want anyone seeing them until they're fully consumed by flames."

Phil and Dwayne made lots of money and died in a fireworks accident on the Fourth of July.

EUPHEMISMS:
THE MARCH OF TIME

As we resume our look at the advance of euphemisms, we have to keep a close eye on the image-makers: advertisers, marketers, public-relations people. And to repeat an earlier point, it's important to remember that, over time, this trend toward softer language has only gotten worse.

It All Got Different

I don't know when the whole thing started, but I do know that at some point in my life, *toilet paper* became *bathroom tissue*. I wasn't consulted on this. I didn't get a postcard, I didn't get an e-mail, no one bothered to call. It just happened. One day, I simply found myself using bathroom tissue.

And then, just as my *loafers* were becoming *slip-ons*, my *sneakers* turned into *running shoes*, and in no time, my running shoes became *athletic footwear*. It was about then that a trip to the department store revealed that my lazy-slob uniform of *sweatpants* and *sweatshirt* were now located in a section called *Activewear*.

The world was changing. I saw *second-hand clothing* referred to as *vintage apparel*; I saw *toupees* advertised as *hair appliances*, in keeping, I would imagine, with the *dental appliances* that had long since replaced *false teeth*.

Ya Gotta Have a System

Of course, if you didn't want to wear a *hairpiece* or a *rug* (nice old-fashioned term), you could always look around for a good, reliable *hair-replacement system*. Keep an eye out for *systems*, folks, they're everywhere. The clerk who sold me my *answering machine* said I was purchasing a *voice-processing system*; a *mattress and box-spring set* is now called a *sleep system*; and the people who sell *mops* have not been resting. According to a commercial I saw recently, the Clorox ReadyMop is now America's favorite *mopping system*.

And if you think you can escape these systems by going for a drive, forget it; your car has been systematically (get it?) infiltrated, too. The *heater and air conditioner* became the *climate-control system*, your *brakes* have been replaced by a *braking system*, and your *seat belts and air bags* are now known as the *impact-mangement system*. You can't beat the system.

Marketers will always strive to make things sound more impressive than they really are; that's why *dashboards* became *instrument panels*. But how's this for laying it on thick? A magazine ad recently informed me that the cars depicted were equipped with leather *seating-surfaces*. When you get right down to it, you have to admit, marketing people have a ton of balls.

That's Entertainment

The upgrading continued: At home, I found myself watching *animation* instead of *cartoons*. And it turns out, all those TV shows I'd seen before were not really *reruns*, they were *encore presentations.* At about that time I noticed *soap operas* had begun billing themselves as *daytime dramas.*

Theaters felt overdue for an upgrade, too, so they became *performing arts centers,* or sometimes *performance spaces*—in keeping with the spirit of certain *nightclubs* who now speak of themselves as *party spaces.* (The really hip just call them *spaces.*) While all this was happening in smaller locations, the big arenas decided they wanted to be known as *events centers.*

Center is another word that's become important. Hospitals have long thought of themselves as *medical centers,* but now libraries have joined the chorus, calling themselves *learning resources centers.* And just to wrap this section up—and returning to show business for a moment—no matter what size the place where entertainment was being presented, at some point it was decided they would all just be called *venues.*

Systems, facilities, spaces, centers, and *venues:* They're all words to keep an eye on in today's atmosphere of increasing self-importance.

You Want More Changes?

Profits became *earnings, personnel* became *human resources,* the *complaint department* became *customer relations.* People started offering *feedback* instead of *criticism; car sickness* turned into *motion discomfort; messengers* became *couriers; junk mail* morphed into *direct marketing; special delivery* was suddenly *priority mail;* and after all these years, I picked up the phone and discovered *information* was identifying itself as *directory assistance.* I don't even want to mention my dismay at the fact that every old-fashioned, shady *used-car* dealer in a plaid jacket was suddenly selling *certified pre-owned vehicles.*

By this time, the *dump* had become the *landfill.* I guess it was inevitable; the *garbagemen* who fill it had long since become *sanitation engineers,* and in some cities, *garbage collection* was going by the fancy (and misleading) name *environmental services.*

The changes even got me where I lived. According to the Census Bureau, my *apartment* had become a *dwelling unit,* and when I asked my *janitor* to put a *peephole* in the door, I discovered later that actually the *custodial engineer* had installed an *observation port.*

Change of pace: One day, a *bucktoothed* girl told me she had *overbite.* That was the day I traded in my *glasses* for *prescription eyewear.*

Of course, some of these language upgrades are more widespread than others; admittedly, they're not all universal. For instance, we still have *motels,* but some of them wanted to charge a little more, so they became *motor lodges.* We also still have *house trailers,* but if they're for sale and profits are involved, they become *motor homes, mobile homes, modular homes,* or *manufactured housing.*

So apparently, what we thought all this time was a *trailer park* is actually a *manufactured-home community.* I guess the lesson is we never quite know what we're dealing with. Could it be that all these years on the *Jerry Springer* show we've actually been watching manufactured-home-community trash?

I Have a Drug (Store) Problem

I guess you've noticed a trip to the drugstore has changed a lot too; the products have all been transformed. To start with, the *medicine* I used to take is now called *medication.* (I have a hunch medication costs more than medicine.) *Mouthwashes* are *dental rinses, deodorants* have been joined on the shelf by *antiperspirants* (probably because *sweat* has become *nervous wetness*), a plain old bar of *soap* these days is being described variously as a *bath bar,* a *cleansing bar,* and a *clarifying bar.* Can you imagine a mother saying, "Young man, if I hear that word out of you one more time, I'm going to wash your mouth out with a *clarifying bar*"? Doesn't sound right, does it?

The hair people have taken liberties, too: *hair spray*—too ordinary. Try *holding mist*. Of course, if you don't want holding mist, you can always turn to *shaping mousse* or *sculpting gel*. Anything to get you to pay a little more. *Cough drops* have grown up and turned into *throat lozenges*, some even calling themselves *pastilles* or *troches*. Guess what? Right! Two dollars more for lozenges, pastilles, and troches.

I can remember, in television's early years, when *constipation* was called *occasional irregularity*. These days, in a kind of minor, reverse-euphemism trend, we're back to constipation, which parallels the recent TV comeback made by *diarrhea*. No more *lower gastric distress*. Diarrhea! "Gotta go, gotta go, gotta go, gotta go!" The new TV candor. (Even though you still can't say *shit*.) By the way, doctors used to claim that constipation could be relieved by eating more *roughage*; now they're pushing *fiber*. I still prefer roughage. If I want fiber, I eat a basket.

And hey, lady! Advancing age causing *vaginal friction*? Tell the pharmacist you have a *personal dryness problem*. I'm sure he has some sort of *intimate feminine-lubricating solution* to recommend. That's the way they describe crotch products now. Even a good old-fashioned *douche* has turned into a *feminine wash*. And remember *feminine hygiene sprays*? Personally, they didn't sound very tasty to me. If they had come in flavors they might have been more successful. Vagin-illa, crotch-ocolate, labia-lime. Just a thought. Anyway, the latest female product I've heard of is *protective underwear*, which, frankly, folks, I don't even want to think about. More later.

CAPITAL PUNISHMENT

Many people in this country want to expand the death penalty to include drug dealers. This is really stupid. Drug dealers aren't afraid to die. They're already killin' each other by the hundreds every day. Drive-bys, turf wars, gang killings. They're not afraid to die. The death penalty means very little unless you use it on people who are afraid to die. Like the bankers who launder the drug money. Forget dealers. If you want to slow down the drug traffic, you have to start executing some of these white, middle-class Republican bankers. And I don't mean soft American executions like lethal injection. I'm talkin' about crucifixion, folks. I say bring back crucifixion! A form of capital punishment the Christians and Jews of America can really appreciate.

And I'd take it a step further: I'd crucify these people upside-down. Like St. Peter. Feet up, head down. And naked! I'd have naked, upside-down crucifixions once a week on TV, at half-time of the Monday Night Football games. The Monday Night Crucifixions! Shit, you'd have people tunin' in who don't even care about football. Wouldn't you like to hear Dennis Miller explain why the nails have to go in at a specific angle?

And I'll guarantee you one thing: you start nailin' one white banker per week to a big wooden cross on national television, and you're gonna see that drug traffic begin to slow down mighty fuckin' quick. Why you won't even be able to buy drugs in schools and prisons anymore.

Personally, I don't care about punishment one way or another, because I know it doesn't do anything. It doesn't really do anything, except satisfy the biblical need for revenge. You know, if you read the Bible, you see it's filled with violence, retribution, and revenge. So capital punishment is really kind of a religious ritual. A purification rite. It's a modern sacrament.

And as long as that's true, I say let's liven it up. Let's add a little show business. I believe if you make capital punishment a little more entertaining, and market it correctly, you can raise enough money to save Social Security.

And remember, the polls show the American people want capital punishment, and they want Social Security. And I think even in a fake democracy people ought to get what they want once in a while. If for no other reason than to feed the illusion that they're really in charge. Let's use capital punishment the same way we use sports and shopping in this country: to take people's minds off how badly they're bein' fucked by the upper 1 percent.

Now, unfortunately the football season only lasts about six months. What we really need is capital punishment year-round. Put it on TV every night with sponsors. Ya gotta have sponsors. I'm sure as long as we're killing people, Dow Chemical and Marlboro cigarettes will be proud to participate. Save Social Security.

And not only do I recommend crucifixions, I'm also in favor of bringing back beheadings. Wouldn't that be great? Beheadings on TV, complete with slow-motion and instant replay. And maybe you could let the heads roll down a little hill and fall into one of five numbered holes. Let the folks at home gamble on which hole the head is gonna fall into. Interactive television snuff-gambling! Give the people what they want.

And you do it in a stadium, so the rabble can gamble on it too. Raise a little more money. And, if you want to extend the violence a little longer—to sell a few extra commercials—instead of using an ax, you do the beheadings with a handsaw. And don't bother getting queasy at this point, folks, the blood's already on your hands; all we're talking about now is a matter of degree. You want something a little more delicate? We could do the beheadings with an olive fork. That would be good. And the nice part is, it would take a real long time.

There are a lot of good things you could do with capital punishment. When's the last time we burned someone at the stake? It's been too long! Here's another form of state killing that comes from a rich religious tradition: burning people at the stake. Put it on TV on Sunday mornings; the Sunday-morning, evangelical, send-us-an-offering, praise Jesus, human bonfire. You don't think that would get big ratings? In this sick fuckin' country? Shit, you'd have people skippin' church to watch this stuff. And then you take the money from the prayer offerings and use it to save Social Security.

And whatever happened to boiling people in oil? Remember that? Let's bring it back. On TV. First you get the oil goin' good with a nice high rolling boil. And then slowly, at the end of a rope, you lower the prisoner, headfirst, into the boiling oil. Boy, you talk about fun shit! And to encourage citizen participation, you let the rabble in the stadium control the speed of the rope. Good, clean, wholesome family entertainment. The kids'll love it. No V-chip to spoil the fun. And all the while they're enjoying themselves, we're teachin' them a nice Christian moral lesson. Boiling people in oil.

And maybe, instead of boiling all these guys, every now and then you could French-fry a couple of 'em. French-fried felons! Or dip a guy in egg batter, just for a goof. Kind of a tempura thing. Jeffrey Dahmer never thought of that, did he?

Jeffrey Dahmer, eat your heart out! Which is an interesting thought in and of itself.

All right, enough nostalgia. How about some modern forms of capital punishment? How about throwin' a guy off the roof of the World Trade Center, and whoever he lands on wins the Publishers Clearing House?

Or perhaps something more sophisticated. You dip a guy in brown gravy and lock him in a small room with a wolverine who's high on angel dust. That's one guy who's not gonna be fuckin' with the kids at the bus stop.

Here's a good one. Something really nice. You take a high-speed catapult, and you shoot a guy straight into a brick wall. Trouble is, it would be over too quickly. No good for TV. You'd have to do a whole bunch of guys right in a row. Rapid-fire capital punishment. Fifteen catapults! While you're shootin' off one, you're loadin' up the others. Of course, every now and then you'd have to stop everything to clean off the wall. Cleanliness! Right next to godliness.

Finally, high-tech! I sense you're waitin' for some high-tech. Here you go. You take a highly miniaturized tactical nuclear weapon, and you stick it straight up a guy's ass and set it off. A thermonuclear suppository. Preparation H-Bomb. Boy, you talk about fallout! Or, a variation: You put a bomb inside that little hole on the end of a guy's dick. A bomb in a dick! And when it goes off, the guy wouldn't know whether he was comin' or goin'! I got a lotta good ideas. Save Social Security.

FARM SYSTEM:
THUGS, PERVS, NUTS, AND DRUNKS

Here's another one of my really good ideas. I'm going to save us a whole lot of money on prisons, but at the same time I'm going to remove from society many of our more annoying citizens. Four groups are goin' away—permanently!

FIRST GROUP: VIOLENT CRIMINALS. Here's what you do: You take the entire state of Kansas and you move everybody out. You give the people a couple of hundred dollars apiece for their inconvenience, but you get them out. Next you put a 100-foot-high electric fence around the entire state, and Kansas becomes a permanent prison farm for violent criminals. No police, no parole, no supplies; the only thing you give them is lethal weapons and live ammunition. So they can communicate in a meaningful manner.

Then you put the whole thing on cable TV. The Violence Network. VNN. And for a corporate sponsor, you get one of those companies that loves to smear its logo-feces all over the landscape. Budweiser will jump at this in half a minute.

SECOND GROUP: SEX CRIMINALS. Completely incurable; you have to lock them up. Oh, I suppose you could outlaw religion and these sex crimes would disappear in a generation or two, but we don't have time for rational solutions. It's much easier to fence off another rectangular state. This time, Wyoming.

But this is only for true sex offenders. We're not going to harass consenting adults who dress up in leather Boy Scout uniforms and smash each other in the head with ball-peen hammers as they take turns blowing their cats. There's nothing wrong with that; it's a victimless hobby. And think of how happy the cat must be. No, we're only going to lock up rapists and molesters; those hopeless romantics who are so full of love they can't help gettin' a little of it on you. Usually on your leg.

You take all these heavy-breathing fun-seekers, and you stick them in Wyoming. And you let them suck, fuck, and fondle. You let them blow, chew, sniff, lick, whip, gobble, and cornhole one another . . . until their testicles are whistlin' "O Come All Ye Faithful." Then you turn on the cameras, and you've got . . . the Semen Channel! And don't forget our corporate sponsor. We're going to let Budweiser put little logo patches on the rapists' pants: "This pud's for you!"

NEXT GROUP: DRUG ADDICTS AND ALCOHOLICS. Not all of them, don't get nervous. Just the ones who are making life difficult for at least one other person. And we're not gonna bother first offenders; people deserve a chance to clean up. So, everyone will get twelve chances to clean up. Okay okay, fifteen! Fine! That's fair, and that's all you get. If you can't make it in fifteen tries, off you go . . . to Colorado! The perfect place for staying loaded.

Each week, all of the illegal drugs confiscated in the United States—at least those drugs the police and DEA don't keep for their own personal use—will be air-dropped into Colorado. That way, everyone can stay stoned, bombed, wasted, smashed, hammered, and fucked up around the clock on another new cable channel: Shitface Central. This is the real Rocky Mountain high.

Now, I've saved my favorite group for last. **THE MANIACS AND CRAZY PEOPLE.** The ones who live out where the buses don't run. And I always take care to distinguish between maniacs and crazy people. A maniac will beat nine people to death with a steel dildo. A crazy person will beat nine people to death with a steel dildo, but he'll be wearing a Bugs Bunny suit at the time.

So you can't put them all away. You have to keep some of them around just for the entertainment. Like the guy who tells you the King of Sweden is using his gallbladder as a radio transmitter to send anti-Semitic, lesbian meat loaf recipes to Marvin Hamlisch. A guy like that, you want to give him his own radio show.

No, the Maniac Farm will be used strictly for hopeless cases. Like a guy who gets a big tattoo on his chest of Madonna taking a shit. You know? Then he tells you that if he flexes certain muscles it looks like she's wipin' her ass. A guy like that, you wanna get him into custody as quickly as possible.

Now, for the Maniac Farm I think there's no question we have to go with Utah. Easy to fence, and right next to Wyoming and Colorado. And Colorado is right next to? Right, Kansas! And that means that *all four groups* of our most amusing citizens are now in one place. Except for the big electric fences. And, folks, I think I have another one of my really good ideas for cable TV. Gates! Small sliding gates in the fences.

Think what you have here. Four groups: degenerates, predators, crackheads, and fruitcakes. All separated by 900 miles of fence. And here's how you have some fun: every ten miles, you put a small, sliding gate in the fence. But—the gates are only ten inches wide, and they're only opened once a month. For seven seconds.

And you know something? Fuck cable, this stuff belongs on pay-per-view. Because if those gates are only open seven seconds a month, you are gonna have some mighty interesting people trying to be first on line. Deeply disturbed, armed, cranky lunatics on drugs! You know the ones: a lot of tattoos; a lot of teeth broken off at the gum line. The true face of America. And every time you open the gates a few of the more aggressive ones are gonna slip through. The crème de la crème. The alphas! They're gonna slip through, they're gonna find each other, and they're gonna cross-breed.

And pretty soon you'll have the American melting pot: child-killers, corpse-fuckers, drug zombies, and full-blown twelve-cylinder wackaloons. All wandering the landscape in search of truth. And fun. Just like now. Everyone will have guns, everyone will have drugs, and no one will be in charge. Just like now. But Social Security will be fully funded.

NOT EVERY EJACULATION
DESERVES A NAME

Have you noticed that most people who are against abortion are people you wouldn't want to fuck in the first place? Conservatives are physically unattractive and morally inconsistent. They're obsessed with fetuses from conception to nine months, but after that they have no interest in you. None. No day care, no Head Start, no school lunch, no food stamps, no welfare, no nothin'. If you're preborn, you're fine; if you're preschool, you're fucked.

Once you leave the womb, conservatives don't care about you until you reach military age. Then you're just what they're looking for. Conservatives want live babies so they can raise them to be dead soldiers.

Pro-life. How can they be pro-life when they're killing doctors? What sort of moral philosophy is that? "We'll do anything to save a fetus, but we might have to kill it later on if it grows up to be a doctor"? They're not pro-life; they're antiwoman. Simple. They're afraid of women, and they don't like them. They believe a woman's primary role is to function as a brood mare for the State. If they think a fetus is more important than a woman, they should try getting a fetus to wash the shit stains out of their underwear. For no pay.

Pro-life. You don't see many white, antiabortion women volunteering to have black fetuses transplanted into their uteruses, do you? No. You don't see them adopting any crack babies, do you? No, that's something Jesus would do.

And you won't see many pro-lifers dousing themselves with kerosene and lighting themselves on fire. Remember the Buddhist monks in Vietnam? Morally committed religious people in Southeast Asia knew how to stage a protest: light yourself on fire! C'mon, you Christian crusaders, let's see a little smoke. Let's see if you can match that fire in your bellies.

Separate thought: Why is it when it's a human being it's called an abortion, and when it's a chicken it's called an omelet. Are we so much better than chickens? When did that happen? Name six ways we're better than chickens. See? No one can do it. You know why? Because chickens are decent people.

You don't see chickens hanging around in drug gangs, do you? No. You don't see chickens strappin' someone to a chair and hookin' up their nuts to a car battery. And when's the last time you heard about a chicken who came home from work and beat the shit out of his hen? Huh? It doesn't happen. You know why? Because chickens are decent people.

Back to abortion: The central question seems to be "Are fetuses human beings?" Well, if fetuses are human beings, why aren't they counted by the census? If fetuses are human beings, why is it there's no funeral following a miscarriage? If fetuses are human beings, why do people say, "We have two children and one on the way," instead of saying, "We have three children"?

Some people say life begins at conception; I say life began a billion years ago, and it's a continuous process. And actually, it goes back farther than that. What about the carbon atoms? Human life could not exist without carbon. So is it possible that maybe we shouldn't be burning all this coal? I don't mean to be picky, I'm just lookin' for a little consistency.

The hard-core pro-lifers tell us that life begins at fertilization, when the sperm fertilizes the egg. Which usually occurs a few minutes after the man says, "Sorry, honey, I was gonna pull out, but the phone startled me."

But even after fertilization it's still six or seven days before the egg reaches the uterus and pregnancy begins. And not every egg makes it. Eighty percent of a woman's fertilized eggs are rinsed out of her body once a month during those delightful few days she has. They end up on sanitary napkins, and yet they are fertilized eggs. So, what these antiabortion people are actually telling us is that any woman who's had more than one period is a serial killer. I don't mean to be picky, I'm just looking for a little consistency.

And speaking of consistency, Catholics—which I was until I reached the age of reason—Catholics and other Christians are against abortions, and they're against homosexuals. Well, who has less abortions than homosexuals? Here's an entire class of citizens guaranteed never to have an abortion, and the Catholics and Christians are just tossin' them aside. You'd think they'd be natural allies.

And regarding the Catholics, when I hear that the Pope and some of his "holy" friends have experienced their first pregnancies and labor pains, and raised a couple of children on minimum wage, I'll be glad to hear what they have to say about abortion. In the meantime, what they ought to do is tell these priests who took a vow of chastity to keep their hands off the altar boys. When Jesus said, "Suffer the little children come unto me," pedophilia is not what he was talking about. He had something else in mind.

SHORT TAKES (PART 2)

**I only respect horoscopes that are specific:
"Today, Neil Perleman, wearing tight-fitting wool knickers,
will kill you on the crosstown bus."**

Sometimes we dismiss something by substituting the letters
"s-h-m" for the initial consonant sound in the word and then
repeating the word itself: "Taxes, shmaxes!" But suppose the
thing you're dismissing already starts with the "s-h-m" sound?
For instance, how do you dismiss a person named Schmidt?

When a ghostwriter dies, how many people come back?

**I'm in favor of personal growth as long as it
doesn't include malignant tumors.**

Whenever I hear about a "peace-keeping force," I wonder,
If they're so interested in peace, why do they use force?

The bigger they are, the worse they smell.

SATAN IS COOL

*Once, at a school function,
I received a dressing down for not dressing up.*

The keys to America: the cross, the brew, the dollar, and the gun.

My watch stopped. I think I'm down a quartz.

A meltdown sounds like fun.
Like some kind of cheese sandwich.

Sex always has consequences. When Hitler's mother
spread her legs that night, she effectively canceled out
the spreading of fifteen to twenty million other pairs of legs.

A parawhore is a woman who keeps you aroused
until they can get you to a real whore.

No one can ever know for sure what a deserted area looks like.

Why don't they put child molesters in a fondling home?

The difference between show business and a gang bang is
that in show business everybody wants to go on last.

Don Ho can sign autographs 3.4 times faster
than Efrem Zimbalist Jr.

The truth is, Pavlov's dog trained Pavlov
to ring his bell just before the dog salivated.

A scary dream makes your heart beat faster. Why doesn't
the part of your brain that controls your heartbeat
realize that another part of your brain is making the
whole thing up? Don't these people communicate?

I never watch *Sesame Street*; I know most of that stuff.

I read that somewhere out west recently a National Wilderness Area
was closed for two days because it was too windy.

We are conditioned to notice and emphasize the differences among ourselves, instead of the similarities. The corporate-style partitioning begins early in life: fetus, newborn, infant, toddler, preschool, lower school, middle school, junior high, senior high, pre-teen, teen. Get in your box and stay there!

> **THE STATUS QUO ALWAYS SUCKS**

Is the kidney a bean-shaped organ,
or is the bean a kidney-shaped legume?

**I like Florida; everything is in the eighties.
The temperatures, the ages, and the IQs.**

*When you cut the legs off jeans to make cutoffs,
don't you feel foolish for just a moment as you
stand there holding two useless denim legs?*

Why does *Filipino* start with an *F* and *Philippines* start with *Ph*?

*I think in retaliation the Jews should be allowed to kill six
million Germans. It's only fair. With fifty years of compound
interest. That would come to about 110 million Germans.
That oughta put a nice dent in bratwurst consumption.*

**I heard about some guy called the Marrying Rapist. He operates
with a minister-partner who performs a wedding ceremony
just before the rape. Police are looking for two men in tuxedos
and sneakers. Possibly carrying rice.**

I think tobacco and alcohol warnings are too general. They should
be more to the point: "People who smoke will eventually cough
up small brown pieces of lung." And "Warning! Alcohol will turn
you into the same asshole your father was."

A fast car that passes you at night is going somewhere.

I recently had a ringing in my ear.
The doctors looked inside and found a small bell.

┌─────────────────────────────────┐
│ **IF IT AIN'T BROKE, BREAK IT** │
└─────────────────────────────────┘

If Frank Sinatra owed you a favor, it would be fun to ask him
to have one of his buddies kill Andy Williams.

**I get a nice safe feeling when I see a police car, and I realize
I'm not driving around with a trunkful of cocaine.**

I'm offering a special prize for first Buick on the moon.

Why do shoelaces only come in certain sizes?

The public will never become concerned about global warming
or the greenhouse effect. These words just aren't scary enough.
Global means all-encompassing, *warming* connotes comfort, *green*
equals growth, and *house* equals shelter. Growth, shelter, and all-
encompassing comfort. Doesn't sound like much of a threat. Relax.

**How can a color be artificial? I look at red Jell-O,
and it's just as red as it can be.**

*Why is it the other side of the street always
crosses the street when I do?*

In Rome, the emperor sat in a special part of the
Colosseum known as the Caesarian section.

**Sometimes, when I'm told to use my own discretion, if no one is
looking I'll use someone else's. But I always put it back.**

┌─────────────────────────┐
│ **BOTHER THE WEAK**   │
└─────────────────────────┘

I don't see the problem with devil worship.

You know what type of cosmetic surgery you
never hear about? Nose enlargement.

My phone number is seventeen. We got one of the early ones.

What goes through a bird's mind when he finds himself
flying through a fireworks display?

If you nail a tool shed closed, how do you put the hammer away?

*Why are there no recreational drugs
taken in suppository form?*

When I'm working, and the television is on, I always tune in
a program I like. If I'm going to ignore something, I want it
to be something I enjoy.

**No one is ever completely alone; when all is said and done,
you always have yourself.**

*I admire an intelligent man with really unattractive, badly
stained and crooked teeth who makes a lot of money and still
doesn't get his teeth fixed. It's an interesting choice.*

Imagine meeting your maker and finding out it's Frito-Lay.

Have you ever groped blindly through the middle of a packed
suitcase trying to find something and then suddenly realized with
horror that the razor blades had come unwrapped?

**I was taken to the hospital for observation. I stayed several days,
didn't observe anything, and left.**

A tree: First you chop it down, then you chop it up.

I'd hate to be an alcoholic with Alzheimer's.
Imagine needing a drink and forgetting where you put it.

Whenever I see a huge crowd, I always wonder how many
of the people have hazelnuts in their intestines.

Sometimes I can't recall my mental blocks,
so I try not to think about it.

*Did you ever notice how important the last bite of a candy
bar is? All the while you're eating it, you're aware that you
have less and less remaining. Then, as you get to the end, if
something happens to that last piece, you feel really cheated.*

> **WOOD KILLS**

If a cigarette smoker wakes up from a seven-year coma,
does he want a cigarette?

There is a small town out west where the entire population is
made up of the full-grown imaginary childhood friends
of present-day adults.

If a painting can be forged well enough to fool experts,
why is the original so valuable?

*Valentine's Day is devoted to love. Why don't we have a day
devoted to hatred? The raw, visceral hatred that is felt every
hour of the day by ordinary people, but is repressed for
reasons of social order. I think it would be very cathartic, and
it would certainly make for an exciting six o'clock news.*

I'm very lucky. The only time I was ever up shit creek,
I just happened to have a paddle with me.

The Japanese culture is very big on martial arts and spiritual disciplines. So when a guy tells me he is studying something that has a Japanese name, I know he has either embarked on a mystical journey or is learning how to break someone's neck with two fingers.

Baseball is the only major sport that appears backwards in a mirror.

> **WHO STOLE THE BANANA GUACAMOLE?**

Virginia has passed a law limiting people to the purchase of one gun per person per month. But if you can show the need for more than one gun a month, you can apply to the police for an exemption. "Listen, officer, we've got a really dysfunctional family here, and . . ."

Why does it always take longer to go somewhere than it does to come back?

People tell you to have a safe trip, as if you have some control over it.

Conservatives say if you don't give the rich more money, they will lose their incentive to invest. As for the poor, they tell us they've lost all incentive because we've given them too much money.

Why is the hot water on the left? I think it's so you can use your right hand to test how hot it is.

People love to admit they have bad handwriting or that they can't do math. And they will readily admit to being awkward: "I'm such a klutz!" But they will never admit to having a poor sense of humor or being a bad driver.

Have you ever noticed that the lawyer smiles more than the client?

E-I-E-I-O is actually a gross misspelling of the word *farm*.

If you can't beat them, arrange to have them beaten.

A recent story in the media said that some firemen in Chicago had refused to enter a burning building because it was too hot.

No one ever mentions when the swallows leave Capistrano.
Do they die there?

The lazy composer still had several scores to settle.

*At what point in his journey does
an emigrant become an immigrant?*

In a factory that makes bathroom disinfectant,
the whole factory smells like the bathroom.

**We have mileage, yardage, and footage,
why don't we have inchage?**

*Travel tip: Economy-section farts on an
inbound flight from the Third World are
the deadliest a traveler will ever encounter.*

Every time you use the phrase *all my life* it has a different meaning.

Great scientific discoveries: jiggling the toilet handle.

When will the rhetorical questions all end?

Why do they call it a garbage disposal? The stuff isn't garbage until after you dispose of it.

A cemetery is a place where dead people live.

Do the people who hate blacks but think they're really good dancers ever stop to think how much better blacks would dance if fewer people hated them?

I do something about the weather. I stay home.

"Let's stop underage drinking before it starts." Please explain this to me. It sounds tricky.

When I'm really bored, I sit home and translate the writing on foreign biscuits.

Political discourse has been reduced to "Where's the beef?" "Read my lips," and "Make my day." Where are the assassins when we really need them?

GANDHI ATE MILK DUDS

Hard work is for people short on talent.

Alter and change are supposed to be synonyms, but altering your trousers and changing your trousers are quite different things.

My back hurts; I think I over-schlepped.

The news story said someone had overcome a fatal disease. Wow!

A Bible makes a delicious meal. Simply rub with olive oil and minced garlic, and bake one hour in a 375-degree oven. Serve with oven-roasted potatoes and a small tossed salad. Serves two. Dee-leesh!

Recently, in a public bathroom, I used the handicapped stall. As
I emerged, a man in a wheelchair asked me indignantly, "Are you
handicapped?" Gathering all my aplomb, I looked him in the eye and
said, "Not now. But I was before I went in there."

**Threatening postcard: "Wish you were here,
but if you come here I will kill you!"**

*I wanted to be a Boy Scout, but I had all the wrong traits.
They were looking for kids who were trustworthy, loyal,
helpful, friendly, courteous, kind, obedient, cheerful, thrifty,
brave, clean, and reverent. Whereas I tended to be devious,
fickle, obstructive, hostile, impolite, mean, defiant, glum,
extravagant, cowardly, dirty, and sacrilegious.*

How is it possible to be seated on a standing committee?

I have come up with a single sentence that includes all of the seven
deadly sins: greed, anger, pride, lust, gluttony, sloth, and envy. Here
it is. "It enrages me that I, a clearly superior person, should have
less money than my neighbor, whose wife I would love to fuck if I
weren't so busy eating pork chops and sleeping all day."

**Recent polls reveal that some people
have never been polled. Until recently.**

*Did you ever run over somebody with your car? And then you
panic? So you back up and run over them again? Did you
notice the second crunch was not quite as loud?*

**If I had just one wish it would be to write
the letter *z* better in longhand.**

Have you noticed, whenever there's a problem in this country they
get a bunch of celebrities or children together to sing a song about
it? Drought, famine, drugs; they sing a song about it. This is an idea
that grew out of the '60s peace movement. The idea then was that if
enough "good" people sang, chanted, and held hands, all the "evil"
people would give up their money, weapons, and power. Worked
great, didn't it?

WE ARE ALL PRECANCEROUS

*I read about a woman who had sixty-three distinct
personalities. Jesus! It would take long enough
just finding out how everyone was feeling in the morning,
can you imagine trying to plan a vacation?*

**I put a dollar in one of those change machines.
Nothing changed.**

After the year 2000, I hope the crime of the century happens real
soon, so I get to read about it.

*They say if you outlaw guns, only outlaws
and criminals will have guns. Well, shit,
those are precisely the people who need them.*

I once found a throw rug in a catch basin.

One time, a few years ago, Oprah had a show about women
who fake orgasms. Not to be outdone, Geraldo came
right back with a show about men who fake bowel movements.

*It is now possible for a child to have five parents:
sperm donor, egg donor, the surrogate mother who carries
the fetus, and two adoptive parents. It renders the statement
"He has his mother's eyes" rather meaningless.*

**The new, modern Swiss Army knife has
an ear-piercing tool and a roach clip.**

One of the best expressions in the English language is,
"Who says so?" I guarantee, if you keep saying, "who says so?"
long enough, sooner or later someone will take you into custody.

*It's hard for me to believe that the small amount of water I
take from the water cooler can produce such a large bubble.*

Infant crib death is caused by grandparents' breath.

I've always wanted to place a personal ad no one would answer:
"Elderly, depressed, accident-prone junkie, likes Canadian food
and Welsh music, seeking rich, well-built, oversexed, female deaf
mute in her late teens. Must be nonsmoker."

I went to the Missing Persons' Bureau. No one was there.

*Beethoven was so hard of hearing
he thought he was a painter.*

I choose toilet paper through a process of elimination.

Meow means "woof" in cat.

On Thanksgiving, you realize you're living in a modern world.
Millions of turkeys baste themselves in millions of ovens
that clean themselves.

A day off is always more welcome when it is unexpected.

Some people see things that are and ask, Why? Some people
dream of things that never were and ask, Why not? Some people
have to go to work and don't have time for all that shit.

RIDE THE WILD PARAMECIUM

*How can everyone's money be "hard-earned," and everyone's
vacation be "well-deserved"? Sounds like bullshit to me.*

What exactly is "diddley squat"?

We now buy watches primarily for their looks, price, or additional functions. The fact that they tell time seems lost.

I think you ought to be able to lease a dog.

I don't understand the particular importance of remembering where you were when JFK was assassinated. I remember where I was a lot of times.

What year did Jesus think it was?

There's a new lottery game called Blotto.
You get drunk and pick the numbers.

With all this natural selection going on, why doesn't the human race get any smarter? Is this it? Why are there still so many stupid people? Apparently, being a real dumb jackoff has some survival value.

Why is there always a small hole near the tip of a pen?

I enjoy going to a party at one of the Kennedys' homes, dropping to the floor, and yelling, "Hit the deck, he's got a gun!"

You know what disease you never hear about? Cancer of the heart.

LIFE IS A NEAR-DEATH EXPERIENCE

Amy Vanderbilt, the foremost authority on etiquette, commited suicide and apparently didn't have the courtesy to leave a note.

If the bouncer gets drunk, who throws *him* out?

The world began going downhill when ticket-takers in movie theaters stopped wearing uniforms.

When primitive people practice the rain dance,
does it rain at the end of practice? And if it doesn't,
how do they know they did the dance correctly?

The original Schick Smoking Centers were very primitive. They
gave you one lecture and then you came back a week later. If they
smelled tobacco on your breath, they beat the shit out of you.

If you live to be a hundred, your lucky number goes up by one.

FUCK THE MIDDLE CLASS

Medical progress: The medical profession is only now beginning
to concede that maybe, just maybe, nutrition has something to
do with good health. And that maybe, just maybe, the mind is
somehow mysteriously linked to the body. Of course, there's not
much money in such thinking.

If you mail a letter to your mailman,
will he get it before he's supposed to?

I enjoy watching a woman with really bad teeth and
a good sense of humor struggling to use her lips and
tongue to hide her teeth when she's laughing. I just stand
there and tell her joke after joke after joke.

Never tell a Spanish maid you want everything
to be spic-and-span.

President Bush declared a National Day of
Prayer for Peace. This was some time after
he had carefully arranged and started the war.

They keep saying you can't compare apples and oranges.
I can. An apple is red and distinctly non-spherical; an orange is
orange and nearly spherical. So, what's the big problem?

After a big flood, where do all those rowboats go?

The Chinese have a saying: On a journey of a thousand miles, 512 is a little more than half.

McDonald's "breakfast for under a dollar" actually costs much more than that. You have to factor in the cost of coronary bypass surgery.

I don't like to lose my bearings, so I keep them in the cabinet near my bed.

When Popeye blows through his pipe, why doesn't he get sprayed with burning ash?

George Washington's brother was the Uncle of Our Country.

If you fall asleep on the couch in a house where a woman is present, there will be a blanket or a coat covering you when you awaken.

Politics is so corrupt even the dishonest people get fucked.

When blowing out your birthday candles, suppose you wish for one candle to stay lit? Is it possible for your wish to come true?

MY FIRST NINE DOGS ARE DEAD

I got a chest X-ray last month, and they found a spot on my lung. Fortunately it was barbecue sauce.

When a masochist brings someone home from the bar, does he say, "Excuse me a moment, I'm going to slip into something uncomfortable?"

This year is the two-millionth anniversary of sperm.

When you pick something up with your toes and transfer it to your hand, don't you feel, just briefly, like a superior creature? Like you could probably survive alone in a forest for a long time? Just briefly.

If all our national holidays were observed on Wednesdays, we might conceivably wind up with nine-day weekends.

The day after tomorrow is the third day of the rest of your life.

Why must hailstones always be the size of something else? And if it must be that way, why don't they have hailstones the size of testicles?

Cloud nine gets all the publicity, but cloud eight actually is cheaper, less crowded, and has a better view.

It is bad luck to kill a dog with a cooking spoon.

Don't you love these people who end their sentences with a rising inflection? And they do it all the time? As though it were an intelligent way to talk? And everything they say sounds like a question? Even the answers? "How are you today?" "I'm fine?"

The swallows know that on the nineteenth of March the tourists come back to Capistrano.

What's all this stuff about retirement I keep hearing on TV commercials? People planning, saving; they can't wait to retire. One woman on TV says to her husband, "At this rate, Jeff, we'll never be able to retire!" What is this all about? Why would someone spend his whole life doing something he can't wait to get away from?

One of my favorite things in the movies is seeing a person hanged.

DON'T GET YOUR CORTEX CAUGHT IN A VORTEX

I often think how different the world would be if Hitler had not been turned down when he applied to art school.

Don't you get tired of these cereal commercials where they show the milk being poured in slow motion, and it splashes off a raspberry?

I enjoy watching people in rush-hour traffic. Thousands of them, stressed, frustrated, hurrying to and from their chosen places of enslavement. It's especially enjoyable from an airplane, because you can see their houses as well. The houses, like the people, all the same. Towns and subdivisions all the same. Cul de sacs. Like their lives, going nowhere. "Not a through street."

I think they should lower the drinking age. I just want to see a sign in a bar that says, You Must Be 11 and Prove It.

Positive thinking doesn't sound like a very good idea to me. I'm sure it doesn't work. And if it does, it's probably real hard to do.

Sometimes when I watch a parade, I wonder how many of the marchers are in desperate need of a good long piss.

So far, the Ku Klux Klan has not produced any really great composers.

THINK CLOWN VOMIT

Tomorrow is very much like today, except it's not here yet.

I admire a man who drives clear across town to a distant shopping center where no one knows him, and rides all afternoon on the children's coin-operated "horsie."

My fondest wish is that I learn to write a capital "X" in longhand without lifting the pen from the paper.

Always be careful what you say. Nathan Hale said, "I only regret that I have but one life to give for my country." They killed him.

**The difference between the blues and the blahs
is that you can't sing the blahs.**

I find the high five repulsive. It's typical lame, suburban white-boy bullshit. Any "five" that takes place above the waist is lame white-boy bullshit. I sincerely hope these high fives are causing long-term arm and shoulder injuries.

> **DOES GOD REALLY HAVE TO WATCH ALL THIS SHIT?**

Bus lag: a low-level disorientation caused by riding on a bus. Almost impossible to detect.

**Long before man discovered fire,
he had sand and water to put it out with.**

*When you look at some of Picasso's paintings,
it makes you wonder what kind of women
he visualized when he masturbated.*

Cancer is caused by a fear of malignant tumors.

Honesty may be the best policy, but it's important to remember that, apparently, by elimination, dishonesty is the second-best policy. Second is not all that bad.

You don't meet many Japanese guys named Biff.

We use the sun to make electricity, and then we use the electricity to operate sun lamps and tanning machines.

I'm unusual in one respect. My lucky number is 541,633.

A laugh is a smile with a hole in it.

People in the central and mountain time zones are getting
too much sleep. Their late news comes on at 10 P.M.,
an hour earlier than in coastal time zones, and yet the morning
talk shows come on at 7 A.M., the same as the rest of the country.
So, central and mountain people are getting an extra hour's sleep.
I think it makes them sluggish.

> **I NEVER LIKED A MAN I DIDN'T MEET**

Preparation H is also good for a fat lip.

It's annoying to have a song running through your mind all day
that you can't stop humming. Especially if it's something difficult
like "Flight of the Bumblebee."

*I'll bet you and I are a lot alike. Did you ever get together
with a bunch of people and hang someone? Isn't it awful?
You just want the guy's body to stop spasming. Every time
I do it, I say, "This is absolutely the last time
I'm doin' this." And still I go back.*

**Most people work just hard enough not to get fired
and get paid just enough money not to quit.**

I recently read that some guy had killed his girlfriend. You know,
it's always been my contention that at the moment you decide to
kill your girlfriend, that decision is tantamount to breaking off the
relationship. Therefore, at the time you kill the person in question
she is actually no longer your girlfriend.

*In reverse order, our last eight presidents: A hillbilly with a
permanent hard-on; an upper-class bureaucrat-twit; an actor-
imbecile; a born-again Christian peanut farmer; an unelected
college football lineman; a paranoid moral dwarf; a vulgar
cowboy criminal; and a mediocre playboy sex fiend.*

I heard that crime has increased so much it is now
a growth industry. My worry is that if it continues to grow
at the current rate it will attract the criminal element.

I read that a Detroit man and his friend were arrested because they
had forced the man's five-year-old son to smoke cigarettes, drink
alcohol, and perform oral sex on them. Can you imagine? Cigarettes!

*In New York State a fourteen-year-old can get married
but he can't drive, so he is forced to go on
his honeymoon on a bicycle or a skateboard.*

SURF'S DOWN FOREVER

There is something refreshingly ironic about people lying
on the beach contracting skin cancer, in an attempt to acquire
a purely illusory appearance of good health while germ-laden
medical waste washes up on the sand all around them.

**The New Testament is not new anymore; it's thousands of years old.
It's time to start calling it The Less Old Testament.**

*I saw a fast-food commercial where they were selling a
sandwich made of pork fat dipped in butter and egg yolk,
deep-fried in lard, wrapped in bacon, and topped with
cheddar cheese. They call it "Plaque on a Bun."*

Crooked judges live on fixed incomes.

In the drugstore, how do you know if you're buying
a sundry, a notion, or an incidental?

Prefix **has no suffix, but** *suffix* **has a prefix.**

*I have no sympathy for single dads. They got into their
marriages because they wanted steady pussy. Steady pussy
leads to babies. After the novelty wears off,
the marriage goes away. Single dads. Big fuckin' deal.*

"It's neither here nor there." Well, folks,
it's gotta be somewhere. I certainly don't have it.

If a really stupid person becomes senile, how can you tell?

Germany lost World War II because Hitler
was completely distracted by ill-fitting clothing that
he was constantly adjusting during the last two years of the war.

The best example of a housekeeper is a divorced woman.

*I read somewhere that in the last census 1.6 percent of the
people were not counted. How can they know that?*

> **MRS. GOODWRENCH IS A LESBIAN**

"Blow your nose" is an interesting phrase. Because you don't
really *blow* your nose, you blow out *through* your nose. If you
blew your nose, I think they'd put you away. You might get
someone *else* to blow your nose, but he would have to be a
really close friend. Or completely drunk.

Just when I began to find myself, depersonalization came in.

*I enjoy making people feel uncomfortable.
Walking down the jetway to board my plane I'll
often turn to a stranger and say, "Boy, I sure hope we don't
crash into a cornfield today. If we do go down in flames,
I hope we hit some houses. Or a school."*

When are they gonna come up with some new Christmas carols?

**You know you're getting old when you begin to leave
the same smell in the bathroom your parents did.**

*Isn't it interesting that only sex and excretion can be
found legally obscene in this country? Not violence, not
neglect, not abuse of humans. Only shitting and fucking;
two of nature's most necessary functions and irresistible
forces. We're always trying to control and thwart nature,
even in our language. Fuck that shit!*

You show me something that doesn't cause cancer,
and I'll show you something that isn't on the market yet.

**Grown-ups have great power. They can order candy
on credit over the telephone and have it delivered. Wow.**

*Heart disease changed my eating habits,
but I still cook bacon just for the smell.*

It has become very easy to buy a gun.
It used to be, "I have a gun, give me some money."
Now it's, "I have some money, give me a gun."

> **YOU ARE ALL DISEASED**

*If you ever meet twins, talk to just one of them.
It drives the other one crazy.*

To promote their hog-raising industry, each year
the state of Iowa selects a young woman and names her
Pork Queen. How would you like to tell the guys down
at the gas station that your daughter is the Pork Queen?

**What exactly is "viewer discretion"? If viewers had discretion,
most television shows would not be on the air.**

*Someday I wanna see the Pope come out
on that balcony and give the football scores.*

A seven-day waiting period for purchasing a handgun is
stupid. It just gives the buyer that much more time to think of
people he'd like to kill. Now, instead of a single murder, you've
got a multiple homicide on your hands.

Have you ever become suddenly, intensely aware of your legs?

> **OUR ONLY HOPE IS INSANE LEADERSHIP**

Remember, inside every silver lining there's a dark cloud.

For the last twenty-five years I've done over one hundred shows a
year, each one attended by about two thousand people. More than
five million people in all. I often wonder if anyone was ever killed
while driving to or from one of my shows. If so, I blame myself.

**Where is this guy Christo when
I need something wrapped at Christmas?**

*I'm not worried about guns in school. You know what I'm
waitin' for? Guns in church! That's gonna be a lotta fun.*

If you look around carefully the next time you go out, you'll notice
that there are some really fucked-up-looking people walking around.

Dogs lead a nice life. You never see a dog with a wristwatch.

*When you close your eyes and rub real hard,
do you see that checker-board pattern?*

If cockpit voice recorders are so indestructible, why don't they just
build an airplane that's one big cockpit voice recorder?

GOOD NEWS: Ten golfers a year are hit by lightning.

*In a trial, if they break for lunch during someone's testimony,
they always remind him afterward that he's still under oath.
That means that all during lunch he was sworn to tell the
truth. So, if someone asks him, "How's the soup?" he better
be goddamn sure he gives an honest answer. "How's the
soup?" "Objection! Calls for a conclusion!"*

I've been working on accepting my inner scumbag.

How do they get all those Down syndrome kids to look the same?

Santa **is** *Satan* **spelled inside out.**

*Don't you lose faith in your dog's intelligence
when he takes a piss and then steps in it?*

There was no Big Bang. There was just a Big Hand Job.

At my supermarket, I get on a checkout line marked "no items,"
and pay for things other people forgot to buy.

*My favorite country song is,
"I Shoulda Fucked Old What's-Her-Name."*

One consolation about memory loss in old age is that you also forget
a lot of things you didn't intend to remember in the first place.

There's actually something called the Table Tennis Hall of Fame.

*Sometimes, during a big funeral that's being shown on TV,
you'll see some really good-looking female mourners. But they
never keep the cameras on them long enough to get a good,
careful look. And you can't see their eyes because a lot of
times they're wearing sunglasses. It's frustrating. I happen to
be particularly attracted to grief-stricken women.*

THE DODGERS EAT SHIT

What year in world history do you suppose the first person with really clean fingernails appeared?

What exactly is "midair"? Is there some other part of air besides the "mid" part?

Singing is basically a form of pleasant, controlled screaming.

The sound of one hand clapping is the same as the sound of a tree falling in the forest when no one is there to hear it.

What clinic did Betty Ford go to?

Wouldn't it be weird if the only way people could die was that their heads suddenly exploded without warning? If there was simply no other cause of death? One day you'd be sitting there having a hot chocolate, and suddenly your head would explode. You know something? I'll bet people would get used to it.

You know what they don't have? Cake-flavored pie.

I'd like to live in a country where the official motto was, "You never know." It would help me relax.

I can't wait until we get a really evil president. Not devious and cunning like Nixon and Johnson. But really, really evil. God, it would be so refreshing!

You know you're getting old when, after taking a leak, you shake your dick and dust comes out.

I avoid any restaurant that features Kaopectate on draft.

Banks tell you to maintain a "minimum balance."
I first learned about minimum balance from my uncle.
He would come over to our house, drink a quart of wine,
and try to stand up. That was minimum balance.

ANOTHER CRETIN FOR PEACE

Every now and then, on certain days, in the late afternoon the air
takes on a weird kind of purply, rose-colored light. What is that?

The neutron bomb is very Republican;
it leaves property alone and concentrates on destroying
large numbers of people indiscriminately.

Being a comedian, I would love to see a production of
Hamlet *that included a drummer, so they could use*
rim shots to highlight the really good lines.
"To be or not to be. That is the question." Ba-dum-dum!

I have no problem with the cigar smoking trend.
If some guy wants to put a big, steaming turd in his
mouth and suck on it, who am I to complain?

Why are we so surprised when terrorists
manage to get a bomb on an airplane?
Drug traffickers get things on airplanes all the time.

When you reach a certain age there
comes a time when everyone you know is sick.

How can people take the Olympics seriously? Judges vote politically,
athletes cheat on drugs, xenophobes run wild, and the whole thing
is one big greed-driven logo competition.

Somehow, it's hard to picture butterflies fucking.

*Do you know the nicest thing about looking
at a picture of a 1950s baseball park? The only
people wearing baseball caps are the players.*

A deaf-mute carrying two large suitcases
has rendered himself speechless.

*It's way beyond ironic that a place called the Holy Land
is the location of the fiercest, most deeply felt
hatred in the world. And it makes for wonderful theater.*

**Whenever I see a picture of the
General Assembly of the United Nations,
I wonder how many of the delegates are whacked on drugs.**

With all the cars, buses, trucks, airplanes, electric motors, gasoline
engines, diesel engines, compressors, turbines, drills, fans, pumps,
and generators running all the time, shouldn't the Earth now be
making a loud humming sound as it moves around the sun?

*The pores in a latex condom are one micron in size.
The human immuno-deficiency virus is one half micron.
So, what's all this stuff about safe sex?*

**Mall walking. How perfect! Staying fit
without having to take your eyes off the merchandise
that got you out of shape in the first place.**

I'm sixty, and I don't need child-resistant caps on my
medicine bottles. They say, "Well, someone with children
might come and visit you." Fuck 'em! They're on their own.
Let 'em take their chances. Anyone who visits me is accepting
a certain level of risk in the first place.

*Can you imagine the increase in violence there would be
if no one could lie? If we could all read each other's minds?
Also, think of all the additional crying there would be.*

A pager is an electronic leash,
the better for your controllers to control you.
One more sign that your life belongs to someone else.

Forty-five million people go to national parks each year.
To get away from the other two hundred million.

Always do whatever's next.

That invisible hand of Adam Smith's seems to offer an
extended middle finger to an awful lot of people.

If you want to know how fucked up the people in this country
are, just look at television. Not the programs, not the news. The
commercials. Just watch only the commercials for about a week,
and you'll see how fucked up the people in this country really are.

Theater and sports are similar, with minor differences:
In theater, after rehearsing, the actors leave dressing
rooms in costume to perform shows on stages in front of
audiences. In sports, after practicing, the athletes leave
locker rooms in uniform to play games on fields in front of
spectators. And although it's true that both fields
have agents, only the theater has makeup.

Sooner or later, your parents die.

Why do they put a suicide watch on certain death row prisoners?
Why would you care if a man you're planning to kill kills himself?
Does it spoil the fun? I also think about the death row prisoner in
Texas who, on the day before his execution, managed to take a drug
overdose. They rushed him to a hospital, saved his life, then brought
him back to prison and killed him. Apparently, just to piss him off.

For many years, the Grand Ole Opry
did not allow drums onstage.

*Life has changed. The stores around the corner
from my house used to be a grocer, butcher, laundry, tailor,
barber shop, shoe repair, dry cleaner, and a beauty salon.
Now it's a wig parlor, karate school, off-track betting,
a software store, sushi, yogurt, video rentals, an adult
bookstore, a T-shirt shop, a copying and printing center, a
storefront law office, and a clothing store for fat women.*

Sometimes, a city describes itself as a "Metroplex." This is one of
those bullshit word formations whereby a community tries to sound
forward and progressive, in spite of all the evidence to the contrary.

**After every horror, we're told, "Now the healing can begin."
No. There is no healing. Just a short pause
before the next horror.**

*I think once people reach the age of forty they should
be barred from using the words girlfriend or boyfriend in
reference to someone they're fucking. It's creepy.*

Attention, all camouflaged males:
In the American Revolution, the militias broke and ran
from battle. They ran home. Only the regular army stood fast.

George Carlin

DON'T BLAME THE LEADERS

You, the People

In the midst of all my bitching, you might've noticed that I never complain about politicians. I leave that to others. And there's no shortage of volunteers; everyone complains about politicians. Everyone says they suck.

But where do people think these politicians come from? They don't fall out of the sky; they don't pass through a membrane from a separate reality. They come from American homes, American families, American schools, American churches, and American businesses. And they're elected by American voters. This is what our system produces, folks. This is the best we can do. Let's face it, we have very little to work with. Garbage in, garbage out.

Ignorant citizens elect ignorant leaders, it's as simple as that. And term limits don't help. All you do is get a brand-new bunch of ignorant leaders.

So maybe it's not the politicians who suck; maybe it's something else. Like the public. That would be a nice realistic campaign slogan for somebody: "The public sucks. Elect me." Put the blame where it belongs: on the people.

Because if everything is really the fault of politicians, where are all the bright, honest, intelligent Americans who are ready to step in and replace them? Where are these people hiding? The truth is, we don't have people like that. Everyone's at the mall, scratching his balls and buying sneakers with lights in them. And complaining about the politicians.

Vote? No!

For myself, I have solved this political dilemma in a very direct way. On Election Day, I stay home. Two reasons: first of all, voting is meaningless; this country was bought and paid for a long time ago. That empty shit they shuffle around and repackage every four years doesn't mean a thing.

Second, I don't vote, because I firmly believe that if you vote, you have no right to complain. I know some people like to twist that around and say, "If you *don't* vote, you have no right to complain." But where's the logic in that? Think it through: if you vote, and you elect dishonest, incompetent politicians, and they screw things up, then you're responsible for what they've done. You voted them in. You caused the problem. You have no right to complain.

I, on the other hand, who did not vote—who, in fact, did not even leave the house on Election Day—am in no way responsible for what these politicians have done and have every right to complain about the mess you created. Which I had nothing to do with. Why can't people see that?

Now, I realize last year you folks had another one of those really swell presidential elections you treasure so much. That was nice. I'm sure you had a good time, and I'm sure that everyone's life has now improved. But I'm happy to tell you that on Election Day I stayed home. And I did essentially what you did. The only difference is when I got finished masturbating I had something to show for it.

THE 20TH CENTURY
WORLD-HOSTILITY SCOREBOARD

The following is a list of hostilities that took place in the 20th Century among the civilized peoples of the world. The uncivilized were unable to provide reliable statistics.

2 world wars

250 civil wars

311 holy wars

1 cold war

516 wars of liberation

331 wars of containment

691 wars of honor

296 declared wars

856 undeclared wars

4 brushfire wars

2 vest-pocket wars

413 limited wars

1,987 acts of war

7,756 warlike acts

88 police actions

2 nuclear attacks

6,578 government massacres

4 holocausts

943 jihads

693 pogroms

614 longterm persecutions

12,111 acts of treachery

575 betrayals of the masses

958 grabs for power

400 putsches

50 total enslavements

837 partial enslavements

4 total genocides

461 partial genocides

13,658 cease-fire violations

3,115 boundary disputes

1,432 border clashes

3,047 social conflicts

798 sectarian rivalries

13,678 civil disturbances

946 carpet bombings

4,288 threats to security

286 popular uprisings

1,877 areas of unrest

622 strife-torn regions

165 internal upheavals

745 political repressions

12,194 acts of sabotage

1,633 swift reprisals

818 armed resistances

639 repressive measures

1,126 violent outbursts

9,876 mass detentions

11,904 guerilla operations

3,466 suicide missions

823 slaughters

1,200 bloodbaths

43,096 atrocities

161 reigns of terror

715 rebellions

28 revolutions

21 counterrevolutions

746 coups

745 countercoups

457 insurgencies

458 counterinsurgencies

4,622 covert operations

3,422 direct interventions

617 enemy incursions

13 measured responses

295 commando strikes

694 retaliatory raids

844 surprise attacks

236 protective reactions

2,155 frontal assaults

213 responses in kind

17,867 hostile incidents

4,756 belligerent moves

938 naked aggressions

849 foreign adventures

601 overseas entanglements

307 arms races

98 international powder kegs

515 regional tinderboxes

818 military flashpoints

2,415 heated exchanges

911 shows of force

668 heightenings of tension

735 deliberate provocations

921 military confrontations

639 dangerous escalations

3,721 terrorist bombings

438 preemptive strikes

630 outside aggressions

8,571 violent disturbances

646 surgical strikes

4,392 diplomatic deadlocks

82,879 ultimatums

788,969,747 heated arguments

823,285,571 shoving matches

917,704,296 fistfights

942,759,050 snotty phone calls

That's how we did, folks. Not a bad record, although we could have done better, considering the number of fools in our ranks.

ROCKETS AND PENISES
IN THE PERSIAN GULF

History Lesson

I'd like to talk a little about that "war" we had in the Persian Gulf. Remember that? The big war in the Persian Gulf? Lemme tell you what was goin' on.

Naturally, you can forget all that entertaining fiction about having to defend the model democracy those lucky Kuwaitis get to live under. And for the moment you can also put aside the very real, periodic need Americans have for testing their new weapons on human flesh. And also, just for the fun of it, let's ignore George Bush's obligation to protect the oil interests of his family and friends. There was another, much more important, consideration at work. Here's what really happened.

Dropping a Load for Uncle Sam

The simple fact is that America was long overdue to drop high explosives on helpless civilians; people who have no argument with us whatsoever. After all, it had been awhile, and the hunger gnaws. Remember that's our specialty: picking on countries that have marginally effective air forces. Yugoslavia is another, more recent, example.

Surfing Unnecessary

But all that aside, let me tell you what I liked about that Gulf War: it was the first war that appeared on every television channel, including cable. And even though the TV show consisted largely of Pentagon war criminals displaying maps and charts, it got very good ratings. And that makes sense, because we like war. We're a warlike people. We can't stand not to be fucking with someone. We couldn't wait for the Cold War to end so we could climb into the big Arab sandbox and play with our nice new toys. We enjoy war.

And one reason we enjoy it is that we're good at it. You know why we're good at it? Because we get a lot of practice. This country is only 200 years old, and already we've had ten major wars. We average a major war every twenty years. So we're good at it!

And it's just as well we are, because we're not very good at anything else. Can't build a decent car anymore. Can't make a TV set, a cell phone, or a VCR. Got no steel industry left. No textiles. Can't educate our young people. Can't get health care to our old people. But we can bomb the shit outta your country, all right. We can bomb the shit outta your country!

If You're Brown, You're Goin' Down

Especially if your country is full of brown people. Oh, we like that, don't we? That's our hobby now. But it's also our new job in the world: bombing brown people. Iraq, Panama, Grenada, Libya. You got some brown people in your country? Tell 'em to watch the fuck out, or we'll goddamn bomb them!

Well, who were the last white people you can remember that we bombed? In fact, can you remember *any* white people we ever bombed? The Germans! That's it! Those are the only ones. And that was only because they were tryin' to cut in on our action. They wanted to dominate the world. Bullshit! That's our job. That's our fuckin' job.

But the Germans are ancient history. These days, we only bomb brown people. And not because they're cutting in on our action; we do it because they're brown. Even those Serbs we bombed in Yugoslavia aren't *really* white, are they? Naaah! They're sort of down near the swarthy end of the white spectrum. Just brown enough to bomb. I'm still waiting for the day we bomb the English. People who really deserve it.

A Disobedient American

Now, you folks might've noticed, I don't feel about that Gulf War the way we were instructed to feel about it by the United States government. My mind doesn't work that way. You see, I've got this real moron thing I do, it's called "thinking." And I guess I'm not a very good American, because I like to form my own opinions; I don't just roll over when I'm told. Most Americans roll over on command. Not me. There are certain rules I observe.

Believe You Me

My first rule: Never believe anything anyone in authority says. None of them. Government, police, clergy, the corporate criminals. None of them. And neither do I believe anything I'm told by the media, who, in the case of the Gulf War, functioned as little more than unpaid employees of the Defense Department, and who, most of the time, operate as an unofficial public relations agency for government and industry.

I don't believe in any of them. And I have to tell you, folks, I don't really believe very much in my country either. I don't get all choked up about yellow ribbons and American flags. I see them as symbols, and I leave them to the symbol-minded.

Show Us Your Dick

I also look at war itself a little differently from most. I see it largely as an exercise in dick-waving. That's really all it is: a lot of men standing around in a field waving their dicks at one another. Men, insecure about the size of their penises, choose to kill one another.

That's also what all that moron athlete bullshit is about, and what that macho, male posturing and strutting around in bars and locker rooms represents. It's called "dick fear." Men are terrified that their dicks are inadequate, and so they have to "compete" in order to feel better about themselves. And since war is the ultimate competition, essentially men are killing one another in order to improve their genital self-esteem.

You needn't be a historian or a political scientist to see the Bigger Dick Foreign Policy Theory at work. It goes like this: "What? They have bigger dicks? Bomb them!" And of course, the bombs, the rockets, and the bullets are all shaped like penises. Phallic weapons. There's an unconscious need to project the national penis into the affairs of others. It's called "fucking with people."

Show Us Your Bush

So, as far as I'm concerned, that whole thing in the Persian Gulf was nothing more than one big dick-waving cockfight. In this particular case, Saddam Hussein questioned the size of George Bush's dick. And George Bush had been called a wimp for so

long, he apparently felt the need to act out his manhood fanta-
sies by sending America's white children to kill other people's
brown children. Clearly the worst *kind* of wimp.

Even his name, "Bush," as slang, is *related* to the genitals
without actually being the genitals. A bush is sort of a passive, secondary sex characteristic. It's even used as a slang
term for women: "Hey, pal, how's the bush in this area?" I
can't help thinking, if this president's name had been George
Boner . . . well, he might have felt a little better about himself,
and he wouldn't have had to kill all those children. Too bad he
couldn't locate his manhood.

Premature Extraction

Actually, when you think about it, this country has had a manhood problem for some time. You can tell by the language we
use; language always gives us away. What did we do wrong in
Vietnam? We "pulled out"! Not a very manly thing to do. No.
When you're fucking people, you're supposed to stay with it
and fuck them good; fuck them to death; hang in there and
keep fucking them until they're all fucking dead.

But in Vietnam what happened was by accident we left a
few women and children alive, and we haven't felt good about
ourselves since. That's why in the Persian Gulf, George Bush
had to say, "This will not be another Vietnam." He actually
said, "this time we're *going all the way*." Imagine. An American
president using the sexual slang of a thirteen-year-old to
describe his foreign policy.

And, of course, when it got right down to it, he *didn't* "go all
the way." Faced with going into Baghdad he punked out. No
balls. Just Bush. Instead, he applied sanctions, so he'd be sure
that an extra half a million brown children would die. And so
his oil buddies could continue to fill their pockets.

If you want to know what happened in the Persian Gulf, just remember the first names of the two men who ran that war: Dick Cheney and Colin Powell. Dick and colon. Someone got fucked in the ass. And those brown people better make sure they keep their pants on, because Dick and Colin have come back for an encore.

THE GEORGE CARLIN BOOK CLUB

> *"We've Got Books Out the Ass"*

OFFER #1: "HOW-TO" TITLES

- *How to Remove Chewing Gum from Your Bush*
- *How to Turn Your Front Lawn into a Cathouse*
- *How to Remove an Infected Cyst from a Loved One*
- *How to Make Two Small Hats out of a Brassiere*
- *How to Make a Brassiere out of Two Small Hats*
- *How to Have Really Nice Lymph Glands*
- *How to Act Laid-Back During a Grease Fire*
- *How to Spot a Creep from Across the Street*
- *How to Dance with a Swedish Person*
- *How to Induce a Clergyman to Grab You by the Nuts*
- *How to Milk a Dog While It's Sleeping*
- *How to Get Through College without Books*
- *How to Make a Small Salad out of Your Work Pants*
- *How to Lure a Weasel into a Cardboard Box*
- *How to Filet a Panda*
- *How to Get a Tan with a Blow Torch*

- *How to Make an Oil Lamp out of Your Genitals*
- *How to Style Your Hair with a Bullwhip*
- *How to Convert an Old Leather Chair into Twelve Pairs of Shoes*
- *How to Achieve Multiple Orgasms with a Pair of Tweezers*
- *How to Kill a Rat with a Paper Clip*
- *How to Lease Out the Space Inside Your Nose*
- *How to Spot Truly Vicious People in Church*
- *How to Become a Total Fuckin' Greaseball*

THINGS THAT ARE PISSING ME OFF

Cigars

Haven't we had about enough of this cigar smoking shit? When are these fat, arrogant, overfed, white-collar business criminals going to extinguish their cigars and move along to their next abomination?

Soft, white, business pussies suckin' on a big brown dick. That's all it is, folks, a big, brown dick. You know, Freud used to say, "Sometimes a cigar is just a cigar." Yeah? Well, sometimes it's a big brown dick! With a fat, criminal-business asshole sucking on the wet end of it!

But, hey. The news is not all bad for me. Not all bad. Want to hear the good part? Cancer of the mouth. Good! Fuck 'em! Makes me happy; it's an attractive disease. So light up, suspender-man, and suck that smoke deep down into your empty suit. And blow it out your ass, you miserable cocksucker!

Angels

What is all this nonsense about angels? Do you realize three out of four Americans now believe in angels? What are they, fuckin' stupid? Has everybody lost their goddamn minds?

Angels, my ass! You know what I think it is? I think it's a massive, collective, chemical flashback from all the drugs—all the drugs!—smoked, swallowed, snorted, and shot up by all Americans from 1960 to 2000. Forty years of adulterated street drugs will get you some fuckin' angels, my friend!

Angels, shit. What about goblins? Doesn't anybody believe in goblins? And zombies. Where the fuck are all the zombies? That's the trouble with zombies, they're unreliable. I say if you're gonna buy that angel bullshit, you may as well go for the goblin-zombie package as well.

Bike Frauds

Here's another horrifying example of a declining American culture. The continued pussification of the male population, this time in the form of Harley-Davidson theme restaurants. What is going on here?

Harley-Davidson used to mean something; it stood for biker attitude; grimy outlaws and their sweaty mamas full of beer and crank, rollin' around on Harleys, lookin' for a good time. Destroying property, raping teenagers, and killing policemen. All very necessary activities.

But now . . . theme restaurants! And this soft shit obviously didn't come from hard-core bikers, it came from weekend motorcyclists. These fraudulent, two-day-a-week lames who have their bikes trucked into Sturgis, South Dakota, for the big rally and then ride around town like they just came off the road. Lawyers and dentists and pussy-boy software designers gettin' up on Harleys because they think it makes 'em cool. Well hey, Skeezix, you ain't cool, you're fuckin' chilly. And chilly ain't never been cool.

The House of Blues

I have a proposition: I think if white people are going to burn down black churches, then black people ought to burn down the House of Blues. What a disgrace that place is. The House of Blues. You know what they ought to call it? The House of Lame White Motherfuckers! Inauthentic, low-frequency, lame white motherfuckers.

Especially these male movie stars who think they're blues artists. You ever see these guys? Don't you just want to puke in your soup when one of these fat, overweight, out-of-shape, middle-aged, pasty-faced, baldy-headed movie stars with sunglasses jumps onstage and starts blowin' into a harmonica? It's a fuckin' sacrilege.

In the first place, white people got no business playing the blues ever. At all! Under any circumstances! What the fuck do white people have to be blue about? Banana Republic ran out of khakis? The espresso machine is jammed? Hootie and the Blowfish are breaking up?

Shit, white people ought to understand . . . their job is to *give* people the blues, not to get them. And certainly not to sing or play them! I'll tell you a little secret about the blues: it's not enough to know which notes to play, you have to know why they need to be played.

And another thing, I don't think white people should be trying to dance like blacks. Stop that! Stick to your faggoty polkas and waltzes, and that repulsive country line-dancing shit that you do, and be yourself. Be proud! Be white! Be lame! And get the fuck off the dance floor!

EUPHEMISMS:
WRITE IF YOU GET WORK

Marx My Words

These days, people who have jobs are called *members of the workforce*. But I can't help thinking the Russian Revolution would have been a lot less fun if the Communists had been running through the streets yelling, "Members of the workforces of the world, unite!"

And I'm sure Marx and Lenin would not be pleased to know that, today, employees who refuse to work no longer go out on strikes. They *engage in job actions* that result in *work stoppages*. And if a work stoppage lasts long enough, the company doesn't hire *scabs*, it brings in *replacement workers*.

Ready, Aim, Non-Retain!

When it comes to firing people, companies try desperately to depersonalize the process so that no human being is ever seen to fire another. The language is extremely neutral, and whatever blame there is goes to something called *global market forces*. Fuckin' foreigners!

And these companies go through some truly exotic verbal gymnastics to describe what's taking place—although I'm not sure it makes the individuals in question feel any better. After all, being *fired*, *released*, or *terminated* would seem a lot easier to accept than being *non-retained*, *dehired*, or *selected out*.

Nor would I be thrilled to be told that, because the company was *downsizing*, *rightsizing*, or *scaling down*, I was part of an *involuntary force-reduction*. I really don't care that my company is *reshaping* and *streamlining*, and that, in order to *manage staff resources*, *a focused reduction* is taking place, and I'm one of the workers being *transitioned out*. Just fire me, please!

I read somewhere that apparently one company's senior management didn't understand the fuss about this issue. After all, they said, all they were doing was *eliminating the company's employment security policy* by *engaging in a deselection process* in order to *reduce duplication*.

P.S. By the way, when those deselected people begin to look for new jobs, they won't have to be bothered reading the *want ads*. Those listings are now called *employment opportunities*. Makes you feel a lot better, doesn't it?

EUInsteinHEMISMS:

EUPHEMISMS:
WHAT DO YOU DO FOR A LIVING?

American companies now put a great deal of effort into boosting their employees' self-esteem by handing out inflated job titles. Most likely, they think it also helps compensate for the longer hours, unpaid overtime, and stagnant wages that have become standard. It doesn't.

However, such titles do allow an ordinary *store clerk* to tell some girl he's picking up at a bar that he's a *product specialist*. Or a *retail consultant*. If it turns out she's a store clerk, too, but her store uses different euphemisms, then she may be able to inform him that she's a *sales counsellor*. Or a *customer service associate*. And, for a while there, they're under the impression that they actually have different jobs.

These are real job titles, currently in use to describe employees whose work essentially consists of telling customers, "We're all out of medium." Nothing wrong with that, but it's called store clerk, not retail consultant, and not customer service associate. Apparently, stores feel they can charge more for merchandise sold by a customer service associate than they can for the same junk sold by a clerk. By the way, if a clerk should be unhappy with his title, he can always move to a different store, where he may have a chance of being called a *product service representative*, a *sales representative*, or a *sales associate*.

And I hope you took note of that word *associate*. That's a hot word with companies now. I saw a fast-food employee mopping the floor at an In-N-Out Burger and—I swear this is true—his name tag said "associate." Okay? It's the truth. Apparently, instead of money, they now give out these bogus titles.

At another fast-food place, Au Bon Pain, I noticed the *cashier's* name tag said *hospitality representative*. The cashier. The name tag was pinned to her *uniform*. The people who sell these uniforms now refer to them as *career apparel*. Or—even worse— *team wear*. I had to sit down when I heard that. Team wear.

Teams are also big in business; almost as big as associates. In Los Angeles's KooKooRoo restaurants the employee name tags say "team member." At a Whole Foods supermarket, I talked to the head of the meat department about ordering a special item; I figured he was the *head butcher*. But his name tag identified him as the *meat team leader*. Throw that on your résumé. I guess the people under him would have been *meat team associates*. I didn't stick around to ask.

So it's all about employee morale. And in a lot of companies, as part of morale-building, the *employees* are called *staff*. But it's all right, because most *customers* are now called *clients*. With those designations, I guess the companies can pay the staff less and charge the clients more.

I'm not sure when all this job-title inflation began, but it's been building for a while. At some point in the past thirty years *secretaries* became *personal assistants* or *executive assistants*. Many of them now consider those terms too common, so they call themselves *administrative aides*.

Everyone wants to sound more important these days:

Teachers became *educators,*

drummers became *percussionists,*

movie directors became *filmmakers,*

company presidents became *chief executive officers,*

family doctors became *primary-care providers,*

manicurists became *nail technicians,*

magazine photographers became *photojournalists,*

weightlifters became *bodybuilders,*

and *bounty hunters* now prefer to be called *recovery agents.*

And speaking of lifting, those *retail-store security people* who keep an eye on shoplifters are known as *loss-prevention managers.* Still more to come. Later.

FAMILIES WORTH LOATHING

Are you sick of this "royal family" shit? Who gives a fuck about these people? Who cares about the English in general? The uncivilized, murderous, backward English. Inbred savages hiding behind Shakespeare, pretending to be cultured. Don't be misled by the manners; if you want to know what lurks beneath the surface, take a look at the soccer crowds. That's the true British character. I'm Irish and I'm American, and we've had to kick these degenerate English motherfuckers out of both of our countries.

But most Americans are stupid; they like anything they're told they like. So when the duke and duchess of Wales or Windsor, or whatever, visit America, and people are asked if they like them, the simpletons say, "Yes, I like them a lot. They're sort of fun." If they asked me I would say, "Well, I'm Irish, and they've killed a lot of my people, so I wish they'd die in a fire. Maybe someone will blow up their limousine."

The English have systematically exploited and degraded this planet and its people for a thousand years. You know what I say? Let's honor the royal ladies: Queen Elizabeth, the Queen Mum, Margaret, Fergie, and all the rest. Let's give them the hot-lead douche. Get out the funnel, turn them upside-down, and give them the hot-lead douche. Right in their royal boxes. That's my message from the IRA to the English.

And I'm really glad the black, tan, and brown people of the world, fucked over by the English for so long, are coming home to Mother England to claim their property. England is now being invaded by the very people she plundered. They're flying, sailing, swimming, and rowing home to the seat of Empire, looking to the Crown: "Hey, mon! What about de food stamps?"

PEOPLE I CAN DO WITHOUT
(PART 2)

- Guys in their fifties named Skip.
- Anyone who pays for vaginal jelly with a platinum credit card.
- An airline pilot wearing two different shoes.
- A proctologist with poor depth perception.
- A pimp who drives a Ford Escort.
- A gynecologist who wants my wife to have three Quaaludes before the examination.
- Guys with a lot of small pins on their hats.
- Anyone who mentions Jesus more than 300 times in a two-minute conversation.
- A dentist with blood in his hair.
- Any woman whose hobby is breast-feeding zoo animals.
- A funeral director who says, "Hope to see you folks again real soon."
- A man with only one lip.
- A Boy Scoutmaster who works at a dildo shop.

- People who know the third verse to the "Star Spangled Banner."

- Any lawyer who refers to the police as "the federales."

- A cross-eyed nun with a bullwhip and a bottle of gin.

- Guys who have their names printed on their belts.

- A brain surgeon with BORN TO LOSE tattooed on his hand.

- Couples whose children's names all start with the same initial.

- A man in a hospital gown, directing traffic.

- A waitress with a visible infection on her serving hand.

- People who have large gums and small teeth.

- Guys who wear the same underwear until it begins to cut off the circulation to their crotch.

- Any woman whose arm hair completely covers her wristwatch.

THE GEORGE CARLIN BOOK CLUB

> *"We've Got Books Out the Ass"*

OFFER #2: ADVICE AND SELF-HELP TITLES

- *Where to Go for a Free Fuck*
- *Eat, Run, Stay Fit, and Die Anyway*
- *You Give Me Six Weeks and I'll Give You Some Bad Disease*
- *Why You Should Never Mambo with a Policeman*
- *The Stains in Your Shorts Can Indicate Your Future*
- *Earn Big Money by Sitting in Your Car Trunk*
- *Where to Take a Short Woman*
- *I Gave Up Hope and It Worked Just Fine*
- *Why You Should Never Yodel During an Electrical Storm*
- *Fill Your Life with Croutons*
- *Six Ways to Screw Up Before Breakfast*
- *I Suck, You Suck*
- *Reorganizing Your Pockets*
- *Where to Hide a Really Big Snot*
- *Why You Must Never Give Yourself a Neck Operation*
- *The Wrong Underwear Can Kill*

- *Now You Can Cure Cancer by Simply Washing Up*
- *Lightweight Summer Ensembles to Wear on the Toilet*
- *Why No One Should Be Allowed Out Anymore*
- *A Complete List of People Who Are Not Making Progress*
- *Where to Throw Up Secretly*
- *Ten Things No One Can Handle at All*
- *Why You Should Not Sit for More Than Six Weeks in Your Own Filth*

OLD AND STINGY

Here's something that pisses me off: retired people who don't want to pay local property taxes, because they say it's not their grandchildren who go to the schools. Mean-spirited retirees usually from out of state. Cheap, selfish, old Bush voters. The ones I read about were in Arizona. AARP members. They take a shit the size of a peanut and think it's an accomplishment.

And it's not like these retirement people can't afford the tax money. Not all old people are as dependent on Social Security checks as they'd like you to think. Some of them get all kinds of checks: Social Security, the VA, private pensions, government pensions. They also have stock dividends, bank interest, and whatever else they've managed to squeeze out of the system.

And still they begrudge their local property taxes simply because their own fucked-up, cross-eyed grandchildren aren't gonna use the schools. Fuck 'em! I say pay your taxes and die like everybody else. I hope they choke on an early-bird dinner.

THE CONTROL FREAKS

Hello. We're the ones who control your lives. We make the decisions that affect all of you. Isn't it interesting to know that those who run your lives would have the nerve to tell you about it in this manner? Suffer, you fools. We know everything you do, and we know where you go. What do you think the cameras are for? And the global-positioning satellites? And the Social Security numbers? You belong to us. And it can't be changed. Sign your petitions, walk your picket lines, bring your lawsuits, cast your votes, and write those stupid letters to whomever you please; you won't change a thing. Because we control your lives. And we have plans for you. Go back to sleep.

UNCLE SAM WANTS YOU

Things I wonder about the FBI's list of the "Ten Most Wanted" criminals: When they catch a guy and he comes off the list, does number eleven automatically move up? And does he see it as a promotion? Does he call his criminal friends and say, "I made it, Bruno. I'm finally on the list"?

How about when a new, really dangerous guy comes along and they absolutely have to put him at the top of the list without delay? (Call it "Number one with a bullet," if you wish.) Doesn't everyone else have to move down a notch? And doesn't one guy get dropped off? How do they decide which guy to drop? Is it automatically number ten? And how does he feel about that? Does he feel slighted? Does he feel maybe it should've been someone else? Has anyone who was demoted ever killed the new guy to gain his spot back?

One last question: Does the FBI search harder for number three than they do for number seven? I would. Otherwise why have the numbers at all? These are the kinds of thoughts that keep me from making any real progress in life.

TOO MANY PEOPLE

There are too many people. Period. There have *always* been too many people. From the beginning. If these diaper-sniffing Christian babymongers would stop having so many of these cross-eyed little kids, maybe the rest of us would have a chance to spread out and have a little fun. Excess children waste our natural resources. If this society wants me to conserve energy, it had better get some of these child-worshipping religious fanatics to stop having five, six or seven babies. When they do that, I'll start turning off the lights. And yes, I know the fertility rate is down. Good. It should go down even further. Every family should be allowed half a child. If that.

POLITICIAN TALK

Politician Talk #1: Term Limits

When people mention term limits to me, I usually tell them the only politicians' terms I would like to limit are the ones they use when speaking. They have an annoying language of their own.

And I understand it's necessary for them to speak this way, because I know how important it is that, as they speak, they not inadvertently say something. And according to the politicians themselves, they don't *say* things, they *indicate* them: "As I *indicated* yesterday, and as I *indicated* to the president . . ."

And when they're not *indicating*, they're *suggesting*: "The president has *suggested* to me that as I *indicated* yesterday . . ." Sometimes instead of *indicating* or *suggesting*, they're *outlining* or *pointing things out*: "The president *outlined* his plan to me, and, in doing so, he *pointed out* that he has not yet *determined* his position."

Politicians don't *decide* things, they *determine* them. Or they make *judgments*. That's more serious: "When the hearings conclude, I will make a *judgment*. Or I may simply give you my *assessment*. I don't know yet, I haven't *determined* that. But when I do, I will *advise* the president."

They don't *tell*, they *advise*; they don't *answer*, they *respond*; they don't read, they *review*; they don't *form opinions*, they *determine positions*; and they don't *give advice*, they *make recommendations*. "I *advised* the president that I will not make a *judgment* until he has given me his *assessment*. Thus far, he hasn't *responded*. Once he *responds* to my initiative, I will *review* his *response, determine my position*, and *make my recommendations*."

And so it is, at long last, that after each has *responded* to the other's *initiatives*, and after they have *reviewed* their *responses*, made their *judgments, determined* their *positions* and *offered* their *recommendations*, they begin to approach the terrifying possibility that they now may actually be required to do something.

Of course, that would be far too simple, so rather than *doing something*, they *address the problem*: "We're *addressing the problem*, and we will soon *proceed to take action*."

Those are big activities in Washington: *proceeding* and *taking action*. But you may have noticed that, as they *proceed*, they don't always *take action*; sometimes they simply *move forward*. *Moving forward* is another one of their big activities.

"We're *moving forward . . . with respect to* Social Security." *With respect to* is lawyer talk; it makes things sound more important and complicated. So they're not *moving forward* on Social Security, they're *moving forward with respect to* Social Security. But at least they're *moving forward*. To help visualize this forward motion, you may wish to picture the blistering pace of the land tortoise.

Now sometimes when they themselves are not *moving forward*, they're moving something else forward. Namely, *the process*: "We're *moving the process forward* so we can *implement* the provisions of the *initiative*." *Implement* means *put into effect*, and an *initiative* is similar to a *proposal*. It's not quite a *measure* yet, but there's a possibility it may become a *resolution*.

Now, one may ask, "Why do we need all these *initiatives, proposals, measures,* and *resolutions*?" Well, folks, it should be obvious by now: We need them in order to *meet today's challenges.* As I'm sure you've noticed, our country no longer has problems; instead we face *challenges.* We're always facing *challenges.* That's why we need people who can *make the tough decisions.* Tough decisions like: "How much money can I raise in exchange for my integrity, so I can be reelected and continue to *work in government?*"

Of course, no self-respecting politician would ever admit to *working in government;* they prefer to think of themselves as *serving the nation.* This is one of the more grotesque distortions to come out of Washington. They say, *"I'm serving the nation,"* and they characterize their work as *public service.*

To help visualize this service they provide, you may wish to picture the activities that take place on a stud farm.

Politician Talk #2: Trouble on the Hill

Continuing our review of the language of the elected, it seems that, linguistically, politicians hit their truest stride when they find themselves in trouble. At times like these, the explanations typically begin with a single word: *miscommunication.*

"How do you answer these felony charges, Senator?"

"The whole thing was a *miscommunication.*"

"But what about the tapes?"

"They took them out of context. They twisted my words." Nice touch. A person who routinely spends his time bending and torturing the English language telling us that someone has twisted his words.

But as the problem gets worse, and his troubles increase, he's forced to take his explanation in a new direction. He now tells us that *"The whole thing has been blown out of proportion."* And by the way, have you noticed with these blown-out-of-proportion people that it's always "the whole thing"? Apparently, no one has ever claimed that only a small part of something has been blown out of proportion.

But as time passes and the evidence continues to accumulate, our hero suddenly changes direction and begins using public-relations jujitsu. He says, *"We're trying to get to the bottom of this."* We. Suddenly, he's on the side of the law. *"We're trying to get to the bottom of this, so we can get the facts out to the American people."* Nice. The American people. Always try to throw them in; it makes it sound as if you actually care.

As the stakes continue to rise, our hero now makes a subtle shift and says, *"I'm willing to trust in the fairness of the American people."* Clearly, he's trying to tell us something: that there may just be a little fire causing all the smoke. But notice he's still at the *I-have-nothing-to-hide* stage.

But then, slowly, "I'm willing to trust in the fairness of the American people" progresses to *"There is no credible evidence,"* and before long, we're hearing the very telling, *"No one has proven a thing."*

Now, if things are on track in this drama, and the standard linguistic path of the guilty is being followed faithfully, "No one has proven a thing" will precede the stage when our hero begins to employ that particularly annoying technique: Ask-yourself-questions-and-then-answer-them:

"Did I show poor judgment? Yes. Was there inappropriate behavior? Yes. Do I wish this never happened? Of course. But did I break the law? That's not the issue."

The calendar is marching, however, and it soon becomes clear that our friend is most likely quite guilty, indeed. We know this, because he now shifts into that sublime use of the passive voice: *mistakes were made.* The beauty of *mistakes were made* is that it doesn't really identify who made them. You're invited to think what you wish. Bad advice? Poor staff work? Voodoo curse?

But it's too late. *Mistakes were made* quickly becomes *eventually I will be exonerated*, which then morphs into *I have faith in the American judicial system*, and the progression ends with that plaintive cry, *whatever happened to innocent until proven guilty?* Whatever happened to innocent until proven guilty; well, he's about to find out.

Eventually, in full retreat (and federal custody), he shuffles off in his attractive orange jumpsuit, and can be heard muttering that most modern of mea culpas: *"I just want to put this thing behind me and get on with my life."* And to emphasize how sincere he is, he announces, *"I'm taking responsibility for my actions."* How novel! Imagine; taking responsibility. He says it as though it were a recently developed technique.

Whenever I hear that sort of thing on the news, I always want to ask one of these I'm-taking-responsibility-for-my-actions people whether or not they'd be willing to take responsibility for *my* actions. You know, gambling debts, paternity suits, outstanding warrants. Can you help me out here, pal?

Regarding this whole put-this-thing-behind-me idea in general, here's what I'd like to do. I'd like to put this I-want-to-put-this-thing-behind-me-and-get-on-with-my-life thing behind *me* and get on with *my* life. May I repeat that for you? I'd like to put this I-want-to-put-this-thing-behind-me-and-get-on-with-my-life thing behind *me* and get on with *my* life.

I think one of the problems in this country is that too many people are screwing things up, committing crimes and then getting on with their lives. What is really needed for public officials who shame themselves is ritual suicide. Hara-kiri. Like those Japanese business executives who mismanage corporations into bankruptcy. Never mind the lawyers and the public relations and the press conferences, get that big knife out of the kitchen drawer and do the right thing.

Politician Talk #3: Senator Patriot Speaks

To take up a thread from an earlier section of this politico-lingo trilogy, we noted at the time the fact that most politicians operate under the delusion that what they're is doing is serving the nation. Of course, if they really feel this way, they're more than simply misinformed, they're obviously not playing with a full bag of jacks.

So, citizens; a question. Do you think it's at all possible that these politicians whose judgment is so faulty that they actually believe they're serving the nation might be expected to indulge occasionally in some, oh, I don't know, exaggerated patriotism? Hah? Whaddya think? Maybe? Hah?

Well, fans, it's not just possible, it's downright inevitable. And should they be so indulging themselves on the Fourth of July, you'll want to be sure to have hip boots and shovels handy, because brown stuff is going to be piling up at an alarming rate. And I suggest you shovel fast, because your elected heroes will be squeezing every last ounce of counterfeit patriotism out of their blood-starved brains.

And so, as you see them rushing madly across the landscape, pushing all the buttons marked red, white, and blue, be on the alert for phrases such as *Old Glory*; *Main Street*; *the stars and stripes*; *the heartland*; *all across this great land of ours*; *from Maine to California*; and, of course, *on American soil*. And don't forget all those *freedom-loving people around the world who look to us as a beacon of hope*. Those, I assume, would be the ones we haven't bombed lately. And you'd also better be ready to be reminded, over and over, that you live in a country that somehow fancies itself *leader of the free world*. Got that? Leader of the free world. I don't know when we're going to retire that stupid shit, but personally, I've heard it quite long enough.

And what exactly is the free world, anyway? I guess it would depend on what you consider the non-free world. And I can't find a clear definition of that, can you? Where is that? Russia? China? For chrissakes, Russia has a better Mafia than we do now, and China is pirating *Lion King* DVDs and selling dildos on the Internet. They sound pretty free to me.

Here are some more jingoistic variations you need to be on the lookout for: *The greatest nation on Earth; the greatest nation in the history of the world*; and *the most powerful nation on the face of the Earth.* That last one is usually thrown in just before we bomb a bunch of brown people. Which is every couple of years. And bombing brings me to the language used by politicians when referring to our armed forces.

Now, normally, during peacetime, politicians will refer to members of the military as *our young men and women around the world.* But since we're so rarely at peace for more than six months at a time, during wars Senator Patriot and his colleagues are fully prepared to raise the stakes. (Don't you just love that word, *colleagues*? It makes them sound so . . . I don't know, legitimate.) And so it is, that in times of combat, our young men and women around the world quickly become *our brave young fighting men and women stationed halfway around the world in places whose names they can't pronounce.* And for added emotional impact, they may also mention that these military folks spend a lot of time *wondering if they'll ever see their loved ones again.* That one gets people right in the belly button. And should the speaker be going for maximum emotional effect, he will deliver the above passage, substituting *sons and daughters* for *men and women.*

And isn't that reference "places whose names they can't pronounce" a lovely little piece of subtle racism? That's an all-American, red-meat bonus they throw in for you.

Here's another way politicians express their racist geographic chauvinism: *young men and women stationed in places the average American can't find on a map.* I've always thought it was amusing—and a bit out of character—for a politician to go out of his way to point out the limited amount of intelligence possessed by the American people. Especially since his job security depends on that very same limitation. It would also appear to contradict that other well-traveled and inaccurate standby: *The American people are a lot smarter than they're given credit for.*

Amazingly, politicians have mastered the art of uttering those words with a perfectly straight face, even though the proposition is stated precisely backward. Judging from the results of focus groups, polls, and election returns that I've seen, and watching the advertising directed at Americans, I'd say the American people are a lot *dumber* than they're given credit for. As one example, just look at the individuals they keep sending to their statehouses and to Washington to represent them. Look also at what they've done to their once-beautiful country and its landscape.

Wrapping up this modest review of patriotic political language, I think it's safe to conclude that the degree of a politician's insincerity can best be measured by how far around the world our soldiers are, and whether or not any of them is able to pronounce the name of the place. And whether or not their neighbors back home can find it on a map.

NOTHING CHANGES

Dear Political Activists,

All your chanting, marching, voting, picketing, boycotting, and letter-writing will not change a thing; you will never right the wrongs of this world. The only thing your activity will accomplish is to make some of you feel better. Such activity makes powerless people feel useful, and provides them the illusion that they're making a difference. But it doesn't work. Nothing changes. The powerful keep the power. That's why they're called the powerful.

This is similar to people's belief that love can overcome everything, that it has some special power. It doesn't. Except one on one. One on one, love is incredibly powerful. It is a beautiful thing. But if love had any power to change the world, it would have prevailed by now. Love can't change the world. It's nice. It's pleasant. It's better than hate. But it has no special power over things. It just feels good. Love yourself, find another person to love, and feel good.

Love, George

THE GEORGE CARLIN BOOK CLUB

OFFER #3: GENERAL INTEREST TITLES

- *Twelve Things Nobody Cares About*
- *The Picture Book of Permanent Stains*
- *Firecracker in a Cat's Asshole: A Novel*
- *The Complete List of Everyone Who Enjoys Coffee*
- *The Official British Empire Registry of Blokes*
- *Ten Places No One Can Find*
- *Tits on the Moon (science fiction)*
- *Why Norway and Hawaii Are Not Near Each Other*
- *The History of Envy*
- *The Pus Almanac*
- *One Hundred People Who Are Only Fooling Themselves*
- *Diary of a Real Evil Prick*
- *Carousel Maintenance*
- *Why It Doesn't Snow Anymore*
- *The Dingleberry Papers*
- *A Treasury of Poorly Understood Ideas*

- *Why Jews Point*
- *The Golden Age of Tongue Kissing*
- *Famous Bullshit Stories of the Aztecs*
- *The Meaning of Corn*
- *Feel This: A Braille Sex Manual*
- *A Complete List of Everything That Is Still Pending*
- *Really Loud Singalongs for the Hard of Hearing*

EUPHEMISMS:
POLITICAL-INTEREST GROUPS

Not all the political manipulation of language is done by the big bad politicians. A lot of it comes from people who think of themselves as good and virtuous: the politically active. Activists. As opposed, I guess, to "passiv-ists." Who should not be confused with pacifists, who are, after all, quite often activists.

God Help Us

Let's start with *faith-based*, which was chosen by right-wing holy people to replace the word *religious* in political contexts. In other words, they've conceded that religion has a bad name. I guess they figured people worry about *religious fanatics*, but no one's ever heard of a *faith-based fanatic*.

And by the way, none of the Bush religious fanatics will admit this, but the destruction of the World Trade Center was a *faith-based initiative*. A fundamentalist-Moslem, faith-based initiative. Different faith, but hey, we're all about diversity here.

The use of *faith-based* is just one more way the Bush administration found to bypass the Constitution. They knew

Americans would never approve of government-promoted religious initiatives, but faith-based? Hey, what's the problem?

The term *faith-based* is nothing more than an attempt to slip religion past you when you're not thinking; which is the way religion is always slipped past you. It deprives you of choice; *choice* being another word the political-speech manipulators find extremely useful.

Choosing Sides

School choice, and the more sophisticated version, *parental choice*, are code phrases that disguise the right wing's plan to use government money to finance religious education. If you hear the word *voucher*, watch out for the religious right. Again, though, be alert for the more sophisticated term for vouchers: *opportunity scholarships*.

It's impossible to mention the word *choice* without thinking of the language that has come out of the abortion wars. Back when those battles were first being joined, the religious fanatics realized that *antiabortion* sounded negative and lacked emotional power. So they decided to call themselves *pro-life*. Pro-life not only made them appear virtuous, it had the additional advantage of suggesting their opponents were *anti-life*, and, therefore, *pro-death*. They also came up with a lovely variation designed to get you all warm inside: *pro-family*.

Well, the left wing didn't want to be seen as either anti-life or pro-death, and they knew *pro-abortion* wasn't what they needed, so they decided on *pro-choice*. That completed the name game and gave the world the now classic struggle: pro-choice vs. pro-life. The interesting part is that the words *life* and *choice* are not even opposites. But there they are, hangin' out together, bigger than life.

And by the way, during this period of name-choosing, thanks to one more touch of left-wing magic, thousands of *abortionists' offices* were slowly and mysteriously turning into *family-planning clinics*.

And on the subject of those places, I think the left really ought to do something about this needlessly emotional phrase *back-alley abortions*. "We don't want to go back to the days of back-alley abortions." Please. It's over-descriptive; how many abortions ever took place in back alleys? Or, okay, in places where the entrance was through a back alley? Long before *Roe v. Wade*, when I was a young man, every abortion I ever paid for took place in an ordinary doctor's office, in a medical building. We came in through the front door and took the elevator. The three of us. Of course, as we were leaving, the elevator carried a lighter load.

A Bunny in the Oven?

Then there's the *fetus–unborn child* argument. Even leaving aside personal feelings, the semantics of this alone are fun to unravel. To my way of thinking, *whatever* it is, if it's unborn, it's not a child. A child has already been born; that's what makes it a child. A fetus is not a child, because it hasn't been born yet. That's why it's called a fetus. You can call it an unborn fetus if you want (it's redundant), but you can't call it an unborn child. Because—not to belabor this—to be a child, it has to be born. Remember? The word *unborn* may sound wonderful to certain people, but it doesn't tell you anything. You could say a Volkswagen is unborn. But what would it mean?

The fanatics have another name for fetuses. They call them the *pre-born*. Now we're getting creative. If you accept pre-born, I think you would have to say that, at the moment of birth, we go instantly from being pre-born to being pre-dead. Makes sense, doesn't it? Technically, we're all *pre-dead*. Although, if you think about it even harder, the word pre-dead probably would best be reserved for describing stillborn babies. The post-born pre-dead.

By the way, I think the reason conservatives want all these babies to be born is that they simply like the idea of birth. That's why so many of them have been *born again*. They can't get enough of it.

Tarzan Would Be Mortified

Here's some more left-wing nonsense, this time from the environmentalists, the folks who gave us the *rain forest*. "Save the rain forest." They decided to call it that because they needed to raise money, and they knew no one would give them money to save a *jungle*. "Save the jungle" doesn't sound right. Same with *swamp*. "Save the swamp!" Not gonna work. Swamp became *wetland*! Nicer word. Sounds more fragile. "Save the wetlands." Send money.

But I think the environmentalists still have their work cut out for them when it comes to *global warming* and the *greenhouse effect*. As I see it, these terms are far too pleasant for people to get all worked up about. For one thing, *global* is too all-embracing for Americans; it's not selfish enough. "Isn't globalization that thing that's been stealing our jobs?" Global doesn't make it. And *warming* is such a nice word. Who wouldn't want a little warming?

Similarly, *greenhouse effect* will never do. A greenhouse is full of plants and flowers, full of life and growth. Green equals life, house equals shelter. The greenhouse effect sounds like something that gives you life and shelter and growth. You're never gonna turn something like that into a villain.

And the environmentalists have another language problem, this one concerning nuclear energy: *meltdowns*. They like to warn us about meltdowns. But a meltdown sounds like fun, doesn't it? It sounds like some kind of cheese sandwich. "Would you like some fries with that meltdown?"

A Few Afterthoughts

Here is more of the distorted language of political persuasion:

- Conservatives oppose *gun control*. Liberals know *control* is a negative word, so they call it *gun safety*. That's about what you'd expect, but it's hard to find words to describe the following distortion: some of the pro-gun people are referring to gun control as *victim disarmament*. Isn't that stunning? Victim disarmament! It takes your breath away. Like a gun.

- Liberals call it *affirmative action*; conservatives are less positive. They refer to *government-mandated quotas*, *racial preferences*, and *unfair set-asides*.

- Rich Republicans want to keep their money in the family, and so the Republican party began to call the *inheritance tax* (a pro-tax term) the *estate tax* (a neutral term), which they later changed to the *death tax* (an anti-tax term).

- When liberals talk about *spending*, they call it *investing* or *funding*. Funding means *spending money*. "We need to do more to fund education." On the other side of the ledger, when Republicans need to *raise taxes*, they call it *revenue enhancement*.

- The energy criminals now refer to *oil drilling* as *oil exploration*. Instead of Mobil and Exxon, they'd rather you picture Lewis and Clark.

- When the original Enron story was developing, Bush's people referred to the crimes as *violations*. They said a *review* might be necessary, but not an *investigation*. So I guess if the other guys do it, it's a *crime* that should be *investigated*, but if your guys do it, it's a violation that should be reviewed.

- Liberals call it *global warming*, conservatives call it *climate change*.

- If you want the individual to sound shady and suspicious, you call him an Eye-racky. If you want to upgrade him a bit, he becomes an *Iraqi-American*. If you're trying to clean him up completely, you call him an *American citizen of Iraqi descent*.

- When people came to this country, primarily from Europe, they were called *immigrants* and *refugees*. As they began arriving from Latin America and the Caribbean, we started calling them *aliens*. Some of them are here illegally. Those in this country who sympathize with that group don't call them *illegal aliens*, they refer to them as *undocumented workers*. Or *guest workers*. Sometimes they're identified by the purely descriptive term the *newly arrived*.

- *Most-favored-nation* trade status was considered too positive a term for China, so it was decided instead to call it *normal trade relations*. Aside from the language, there is no difference between the two policies.

- The Nazis referred to the extermination of the Jews as *special action*. In their version, the Jews were not killed, they were *resettled*, *evacuated*, or *transferred*. The dead were referred to as the *no longer relevant*.

- In Palestine, Arabs refer to the areas Jews have taken over as *occupied territories*. Jews call them *disputed areas*.

The Israelis call their assassinations of Palestinian leaders *focused thwartings, pinpoint elimination,* and *preventive measures.*

- At one time in Iraq Hussein called the hostages he was holding his *guests.*

- Countries we used to call *rogue nations* are now referred to as *nations of concern,* so we can talk with them without insulting them outright. But as a result of bad behavior, North Korea has been downgraded from a *state of concern* to a *rogue state.* Likewise, *failed nations* are now called *messy states. Underdeveloped countries* have also been upgraded. They're now *developing nations.*

And finally . . .

- During the election that defeated Manuel Noriega in Panama, there were groups of thugs that wandered around beating and killing people and looting stores. They called themselves *dignity battalions.*

A PLACE FOR YOUR STUFF

Hi! How are ya? You got your stuff with you? I'll bet you do. Guys have stuff in their pockets; women have stuff in their purses. Of course, some women have pockets, and some guys have purses. That's okay. There's all different ways of carryin' your stuff.

Then there's all the stuff you have in your car. You got stuff in the trunk. Lotta different stuff: spare tire, jack, tools, old blanket, extra pair of sneakers. Just in case you wind up barefoot on the highway some night.

And you've got other stuff in your car. In the glove box. Stuff you might need in a hurry: flashlight, map, sunglasses, automatic weapon. You know. Just in case you wind up barefoot on the highway some night.

So stuff is important. You gotta take care of your stuff. You gotta have a *place* for your stuff. Everybody's gotta have a place for their stuff. That's what life is all about, tryin' to find a place for your stuff! That's all your house is: a place to keep your stuff. If you didn't have so much stuff, you wouldn't *need* a house. You could just walk around all the time.

A house is just a pile of stuff with a cover on it. You can see that when you're taking off in an airplane. You look down and see all the little piles of stuff. Everybody's got his own little pile of stuff. And they lock it up! That's right! When you leave your house, you gotta lock it up. Wouldn't want somebody to come by and *take* some of your stuff. 'Cause they always take the *good* stuff! They don't bother with that crap you're saving. Ain't nobody interested in your fourth-grade arithmetic papers. *National Geographics*, commemorative plates, your prize collection of Navajo underwear; they're not interested. They just want the good stuff; the shiny stuff; the electronic stuff.

So when you get right down to it, your house is nothing more than a place to keep your stuff . . . while you go out and get . . . *more stuff*. 'Cause that's what this country is all about. Tryin' to get more stuff. Stuff you don't want, stuff you don't need, stuff that's poorly made, stuff that's overpriced. Even stuff you can't afford! Gotta keep on gettin' more stuff. Otherwise someone else might wind up with more stuff. Can't let that happen. Gotta have the most stuff.

So you keep gettin' more and more stuff, and puttin' it in different places. In the closets, in the attic, in the basement, in the garage. And there might even be some stuff you left at your parents' house: baseball cards, comic books, photographs, souvenirs. Actually, your parents threw that stuff out long ago.

So now you got a houseful of stuff. And, even though you might like your house, you gotta move. Gotta get a bigger house. Why? Too much stuff! And that means you gotta move all your stuff. Or maybe, put some of your stuff in storage. Storage! Imagine that. There's a whole industry based on keepin' an eye on other people's stuff.

Or maybe you could sell some of your stuff. Have a yard sale, have a garage sale! Some people drive around all weekend just lookin' for garage sales. They don't have enough of their own stuff, they wanna buy other people's stuff.

Or you could take your stuff to the swap meet, the flea market, the rummage sale, or the auction. There's a lotta ways to get rid of stuff. You can even give your stuff away. The Salvation Army and Goodwill will actually come to your house and pick up your stuff and give it to people who don't have much stuff. It's part of what economists call the Redistribution of Stuff.

OK, enough about your stuff. Let's talk about other people's stuff. Have you ever noticed when you visit someone else's house, you never quite feel at home? You know why? No room for your stuff! Somebody *else's* stuff is all over the place. And what crummy stuff it is! "God! Where'd they get *this* stuff?"

And you know how sometimes when you're visiting someone, you unexpectedly have to stay overnight? It gets real late, and you decide to stay over? So they put you in a bedroom they don't use too often . . . because Grandma died in it eleven years ago! And they haven't moved any of her stuff? Not even the vaporizer?

Or whatever room they put you in, there's usually a dresser or a nightstand, and there's never any room on it for your stuff. Someone else's shit is on the dresser! Have you noticed that their stuff is shit, and your shit is stuff? "Get this shit off of here, so I can put my stuff down!" Crap is also a form of stuff. Crap is the stuff that belongs to the person you just broke up with. "When are you comin' over here to pick up the rest of your crap?"

Now, let's talk about traveling. Sometimes you go on vacation, and you gotta take some of your stuff. Mostly stuff to wear. But which stuff should you take? Can't take all your stuff. Just the stuff you really like; the stuff that fits you well that month. In effect, on vacation, you take a smaller, "second version" of your stuff.

Let's say you go to Honolulu for two weeks. You gotta take two big suitcases of stuff. Two weeks, two big suitcases. That's the stuff you check onto the plane. But you also got your carry-on stuff, plus the stuff you bought in the airport. So now you're all set to go. You got stuff in the overhead rack, stuff under the seat, stuff in the seat pocket, and stuff in your lap. And let's not forget the stuff you're gonna steal from the airline: silverware, soap, blanket, toilet paper, salt and pepper shakers. Too bad those headsets won't work at home.

And so you fly to Honolulu, and you claim your stuff—if the airline didn't drop it in the ocean—and you go to the hotel, and the first thing you do is put away your stuff. There's lots of places in a hotel to put your stuff.

"I'll put some stuff in here, you put some stuff in there. Hey, don't put your stuff in *there*! That's my stuff! Here's another place! Put some stuff in here. And there's another place! Hey, you know what? We've got more places than we've got stuff! We're gonna hafta go out and buy . . . *more stuff*!!!"

Finally you put away all your stuff, but you don't quite feel at ease, because you're a long way from home. Still, you sense that you must be OK, because you do have some of your stuff with you. And so you relax in Honolulu on that basis. That's when your friend from Maui calls and says, "Hey, why don't you come over to Maui for the weekend and spend a couple of nights over here?"

Oh no! Now whaddya bring? Can't bring all this stuff. You gotta bring an even *smaller* version of your stuff. Just enough stuff for a weekend on Maui. The "third version" of your stuff.

And, as you're flyin' over to Maui, you realize that you're really spread out now: You've got stuff all over the world!! Stuff at home, stuff in the garage, stuff at your parents' house (maybe), stuff in storage, stuff in Honolulu, and stuff on the plane. Supply lines are getting longer and harder to maintain!

Finally you get to your friends' place on Maui, and they give you a little room to sleep in, and there's a nightstand. Not much room on it for your stuff, but it's OK because you don't have much stuff now. You got your 8 x 10 autographed picture of Drew Carey, a large can of gorgonzola-flavored Cheez Whiz, a small, unopened packet of brown confetti, a relief map of Corsica, and a family-size jar of peppermint-flavored, petrified egg whites. And you know that even though you're a long way from home, you must be OK because you do have a good supply of peppermint-flavored, petrified egg whites. And so you begin to relax in Maui on that basis. That's when your friend says, "Hey, I think tonight we'll go over to the other side of the island and visit my sister. Maybe spend the night over there."

Oh no! Now whaddya bring? Right! You gotta bring an even smaller version. The "fourth version" of your stuff. Just the stuff you *know* you're gonna need: Money, keys, comb, wallet, lighter, hankie, pen, cigarettes, contraceptives, Vaseline, whips, chains, whistles, dildos, and a book. Just the stuff you *hope* you're gonna need. Actually, your friend's sister probably has her own dildos.

By the way, if you go to the beach while you're visiting the sister, you're gonna have to bring—that's right—an even smaller version of your stuff: the "fifth version." Cigarettes and wallet. That's it. You can always borrow someone's suntan lotion. And then suppose, while you're there on the beach, you decide to walk over to the refreshment stand to get a hot dog? That's right, my friend! Number six! The most important version of your stuff: your wallet! Your wallet contains the only stuff you really can't do without.

Well, by the time you get home you're pretty fed up with your stuff and all the problems it creates. And so about a week later, you clean out the closet, the attic, the basement, the garage, the storage locker, and all the other places you keep your stuff, and you get things down to manageable proportions. Just the right amount of stuff to lead a simple and uncomplicated life. And that's when the phone rings. It's a lawyer. It seems your aunt has died . . . and left you all her stuff. Oh no! Now whaddya do? Right. You do the only thing you can do. The honorable thing. You tell the lawyer to stuff it.

SMALL TOWNS

You know you're in a small town when:

- The restaurant closes at lunch so the waitress can go home and eat.

- The mayor's nickname is "Greasy Dick" and besides appearing on the ballot, it also appears on his driver's license.

- The fashion boutique/post office is located in one corner of the hardware store between the used milking machines and the pay toilet.

- The police station is closed evenings and weekends, but they leave lit the sign that gives the time and temperature.

- The newspaper prints the crossword puzzle on the front page above the fold, and prints the answers just below.

- The zip code has three digits and features a decimal point.

- The Narcotics Anonymous chapter has only one member, and he's strung out on ranch dressing.

EXPRESSIONS I QUESTION
(PART 2)

There are many expressions we take for granted. We use them all the time, yet never examine them carefully. We just say them as if they really made sense.

LEGALLY DRUNK. Well, if it's legal, what's the problem? "Leave me alone, officer, I'm legally drunk!"

YOU KNOW WHERE YOU CAN STICK IT. Why do we assume everyone knows where they can stick it? Suppose you don't know? Suppose you're a new guy, and you have absolutely no idea where you can stick it? I think there ought to be a government booklet entitled *Where to Stick It*. Now that I think of it, I believe there *is* a government booklet like that. They send it to you on April 15.

UNDISPUTED HEAVYWEIGHT CHAMPION. Well, if it's undisputed what's all the fighting about? To me, "undisputed" means we all agree. Here you have two men beating the shit out of one another over something they apparently agree on. Makes no sense.

IT'S THE QUIET ONES YOU GOTTA WATCH. Every time I see a television news story about a mass murderer, the guy's neighbor always says, "Well, he was very quiet." And someone I'm with says, "It's the quiet ones you gotta watch."

This sounds like a very dangerous assumption. I'll bet anything that while you're busy watching a quiet one, a noisy one will kill you.

Suppose you're in a bar, and one guy is sitting over on the side, reading a book, not bothering anybody. And another guy is standing up at the front, bangin' a machete on the bar, screamin', "I'm gonna kill the next motherfucker who pisses me off!"

Who you gonna watch?

LOCK HIM UP AND THROW AWAY THE KEY. This is one you hear a lot from men. Men like to talk that way; it makes 'em feel tough. A guy sees a rapist on the TV news, he says, "You see that guy? They oughta lock him up, and throw away the key."

This is really stupid. First of all, every time the guy's gotta take a shit, you're gonna have to call the locksmith. If he's in prison thirty years, even if he's eatin' government cheese, it's gonna cost you a fortune.

Second, where do you throw the key? Right out in front of the jail? His friends'll find it! How far can you throw a key? Fifty, sixty feet the most. Even if you hold it flat on its side and scale it, whaddaya get? An extra ten feet, tops! This is a stupid idea that needs to be completely rethought.

DOWN THE TUBES. That's one you hear a lot. People say, "This country is goin' down the tubes." What tubes? Have you seen any tubes? Where are these tubes? And where do they go? And how come there's more than one tube? It would seem to me for one country all you need is one tube. Does every state have to have its own tube? One tube is all you need.

But a tube that big? Somebody would have seen it by now. Somebody would've said, "Hey, Joey! Lookit the fuckin' tube! Big-ass fuckin' tube, over here!" You never hear that. You know why? No tubes! We don't have tube one. We are, sorry to say, tubeless.

TAKES THE CAKE. "Boy, he really takes the cake." Where? Where do you take a cake? To the movies? You know where I would take a cake? Down to the bakery, to see the other cakes. And how come he takes the cake? How come he doesn't take the pie? A pie is easier to carry than a cake. "Easy as pie." A cake is not too hard to carry, either. "Piece of cake."

THE GREATEST THING SINCE SLICED BREAD. So this is it? A couple of hundred thousand years . . . sliced bread? What about the Pyramids? The Panama Canal? The Great Wall of China? Even a lava lamp, to me, is greater than sliced bread. What's so great about sliced bread? You got a knife, you got a loaf of bread. Slice the fuckin' thing!! And get on with your life.

OUT WALKING THE STREETS. This is another one you hear from men. Some guy sees a rapist on the news. Same rapist as before; only this time he's being released. The guy says, "You see that? You see that guy? They're lettin' him go! Now, instead of bein' in prison, he's out walkin' the streets!"

How do we know? How do we know he's out walkin' the streets? Maybe he's home bangin' the baby-sitter. Not every-body who gets a parole is out walkin' the streets. A lot of times they steal a car. We oughta be glad. "Thank God he stole a car. At least he's not out walkin' the streets."

FINE AND DANDY. That's an old-fashioned one, isn't it? You say to a guy, "How are ya?" He says, "Fine and dandy." Not me. I never say that. You know why? Because I'm never both those things at the same time. Sometimes I'm fine. But I'm not dandy. I might be close to dandy. I might be approaching dandy. I might even be in the general vicinity of dandy-hood. But not quite fully dandy. Other times, I might indeed be highly dandy. However, not fine. One time, 1978. August. For about an hour. I was both fine and dandy at the same time. But nobody asked me how I was. I coulda told 'em, "Fine and dandy!" I consider it a lost opportunity.

WALKING PAPERS. Some guy gets fired, they say, "Well, they gave him his walkin' papers today." Lemme ask you something. Did you ever get any walking papers? Seriously? Believe me, in my life I got fired a lot of times. I never got any walkin' papers. I never got a pink slip, either. You know what I would get? A guy would come around to my desk and say, "Get the fuck outta here!!" You don't need paper for that.

THE RIOT ACT. They keep saying they're going to read that to you. Tell the truth, have you heard this thing at all? Ever?

It's especially a problem when you're a kid. They like to threaten you.

"You wait'll your father comes home. He's gonna read you the riot act!"

"Oh yeah? Well, tell him I already read it myself! And I didn't like it! I consider it wordy and poorly thought out. If he wants to read me somethin', how about *The Gentleman's Guide to the Golden Age of Tongue-Kissing?*

MORE THAN HAPPY. I'll bet you say that sometimes. I'll bet you say, "Oh, I'd be more than happy to do that." How can you be more than happy? To me, this sounds like a dangerous mental condition. "We had to put Laszlo under physical restraint; he was . . . well, he was more than happy."

One more of these expressions: **IN YOUR OWN WORDS.** You hear it in classrooms. And courtrooms. They'll say, "Tell us . . . in your own words . . ." Do you have your own words? Personally, I'm using the ones everybody else has been using. Next time they tell you to say something in your own words, say, "Nigflot blorny quando floon."

SHORT TAKES (PART 3)

I don't hear much of that elevator music anymore.
What's going on?

> IT'S TIME TO START SLAPPING PEOPLE

Don't you think there were probably a lot of singers with
great voices who never got famous because they were
too ugly to stand up and be seen in public?

*I can't wait to see one of those actor-assholes
who drive race cars get killed on TV.*

Why do women wear evening gowns to nightclubs?
Why don't they wear nightgowns?

I think many years ago an advanced civilization intervened with
us genetically and gave us just enough intelligence to develop
dangerous technology but not enough to use it wisely. Then they
sat back to watch the fun. Kind of like a human zoo. And you
know what? They're getting their money's worth.

After you die, your "stuff" becomes your "personal effects."

GOD BLESS US ALL. RIGHT IN THE MOUTH

**I think people should be allowed to do anything they want.
We haven't tried that for a while. Maybe this time it'll work.**

People ask me if I have an e-mail address, and I say,
"www.fuckyou.com@blowme/upyourass."
And they seem to understand.

*Message to the Denver Nuggets regarding Columbine High
School: There's no reason to cancel a sporting event just
because some kids kill each other. Try to concentrate on
basketball and leave the life-and-death shit to someone else.*

**Capitalism tries for a delicate balance: It attempts to work things
out so that everyone gets just enough stuff to keep them from
getting violent and trying to take other people's stuff.**

Baseball bats are now the preferred weapon for many
drug gangs and others who have a business need to administer
behavioral reminders. They're cheap, lethal, legal, untraceable,
and hey! It's the national pastime.

**Dying must have survival value.
Or it wouldn't be part of the biological process.**

*Why is it that, when making reference to something in
the past, people often think they have to say, "I hope I'm
not dating myself"? Listen, if you're so embarrassed by
your age there's a simple solution: open a vein.*

I don't have hobbies, I have interests. Hobbies cost money.
Interests are free.

With all the presidential administrations we've had, I'm sure that by now there must have been at least one person who, besides being in the cabinet, was also in the closet.

I don't like it when I'm in an audience and the emcee tells us to give someone a welcome specific to that city: "Let's all get together and give this little lady a nice Toledo welcome." I've often thought if I were from Toledo it would be fun now and then to give someone a Baltimore welcome, just to break the emcee's balls. Or maybe slip in an exotic Budapest welcome when no one is expecting it. One thing I would never do is give someone a Dallas welcome. That's what JFK got. Dallas welcomes don't last too long.

You rarely see an elderly midget.
Apparently their life spans are shorter too.

A PEAR IS A FAILED APPLE

You keep hearing that society's greatest tasks are educating people and getting them jobs. That's great. Two things people hate to do: go to school and go to work.

We busy ourselves with meaningless gestures such as Take Our Daughters to Work Day, which applies primarily to white, middle-class daughters. More help for the wrong people.

People seem to think that if there's some problem that makes them unhappy in this country, all they have to do is stage a big march and everything will change. When will they learn?

Complaint: Where did this dumb-ass Sammy Sosa thumping-your-chest, kissing-your-fingers, flashing-the-peace-sign nonsense come from? What's that stupid shit all about? Geraldo does a variation on it. It strikes me as pretentious, meaningless, pseudoreligious bullshit.

I don't know about you, but I really have no problem with atrocities. What's the big deal? Lighten up.

Can placebos cause side effects?
If so, are the side effects real?

When hundreds of people are killed in an airplane crash I always wonder if maybe there wasn't one guy, a little behind schedule that day, who ran down the last few hundred yards of the airport concourse to make the plane on time. And when he finally sat down in his seat, out of breath, he was really glad he made it. And then an hour later the plane goes down. What goes through his mind? Do you think maybe in those last few moments, as he plunges to the Earth he wishes he'd had a heart attack while running through the airport?

Why do they bother with a suicide watch when
someone is on death row? "Keep an eye on this guy.
We're gonna kill him, and we don't want him to hurt himself."

I notice at Jewish weddings they break a glass. You ever been to an Irish wedding? Glasses, bottles, mirrors, tables, chairs, arms, legs, the band instruments, and the groom's neck. We don't fuck around. Mazel tov!

BASEBALL AND FOOTBALL

Baseball is different from any other sport; very different.

For instance, in most sports you score points or goals; in baseball you score runs.

In most sports the ball, or object, is put in play by the offensive team; in baseball the defensive team puts the ball in play, and only the defense is allowed to touch the ball. In fact, in baseball if an offensive player touches the ball intentionally, he's out; sometimes unintentionally, he's out.

Also: In football, basketball, soccer, volleyball, and all other sports played with a ball, you score *with* the ball, and without the ball you can't score. In baseball the ball prevents you from scoring.

In most sports the team is run by a coach; in baseball the team is run by a manager; and only in baseball does the manager (or coach) wear the same clothing the players do. If you had ever seen John Madden in his Oakland Raiders football uniform, you would know the reason for this custom.

Now, I've mentioned football. Baseball and football are the two most popular spectator sports in this country. And, as such, it seems they ought to be able to tell us something about ourselves and our values. And maybe how those values have changed over the last 150 years. For those reasons, I enjoy comparing baseball and football:

Baseball is a nineteenth-century pastoral game.
Football is a twentieth-century technological struggle.

Baseball is played on a diamond, in a park. The baseball park!
Football is played on a gridiron, in a stadium, sometimes called Soldier Field or War Memorial Stadium.

Baseball begins in the spring, the season of new life.
Football begins in the fall, when everything is dying.

In football you wear a helmet.
In baseball you wear a cap.

Football is concerned with *downs*. "What down is it?"
Baseball is concerned with *ups*. "Who's up? Are you up? I'm not up! He's up!"

In football you receive a penalty.
In baseball you make an error.

In football the specialist comes in to kick.
In baseball the specialist comes in to relieve somebody.

Football has hitting, clipping, spearing, piling on, personal fouls, late hitting, and unnecessary roughness.
Baseball has the sacrifice.

Football is played in any kind of weather: Rain, snow, sleet, hail, fog . . . can't see the game, don't know if there is a game going on; mud on the field . . . can't read the uniforms, can't read the yard markers, the struggle will continue!

In baseball if it rains, we don't go out to play. "I can't go out! It's raining out!"

Baseball has the seventh-inning stretch.
Football has the two-minute warning.

Baseball has no time limit: "We don't know when it's gonna end!" Football is rigidly timed, and it will end "even if we have to go to sudden death."

In baseball, during the game, in the stands, there's a kind of picnic feeling. Emotions may run high or low, but there's not that much unpleasantness.

In football, during the game in the stands, you can be sure that at least twenty-seven times you were perfectly capable of taking the life of a fellow human being.

And finally, the objectives of the two games are completely different:

In football the object is for the quarterback, otherwise known as the field general, to be on target with his aerial assault, riddling the defense by hitting his receivers with deadly accuracy in spite of the blitz, even if he has to use the shotgun. With short bullet passes and long bombs, he marches his troops into enemy territory, balancing this aerial assault with a sustained ground attack that punches holes in the forward wall of the enemy's defensive line.

In baseball the object is to go home! And to be safe! "I hope I'll be safe at home!"

ERIN GO FUCK YOURSELF

Being Irish, I guess I should resent the Notre Dame nickname, "The Fighting Irish." After all, how long do you think nicknames like "The Bargaining Jews" or "The Murdering Italians" would last? Only the ironic Irish could be so naively honest. I get the feeling that Notre Dame came real close to naming itself "The Fuckin' Drunken, Thick-skulled, Brawling, Short-dicked Irish."

PLAY BALL!!!

Here's something I don't care about: athlete's families. This is really the bottom of the sports barrel. I'm watchin' a ballgame, and just because some athlete's wife is in the stands, someone thinks they have to put her picture on the screen. And I miss a double steal! Same with a ballplayer's father. Goddamn! "There's his dad, who taught him how to throw the changeup when he was two years old." Fuck him, the sick bastard! His own sports dreams probably crash-landed, so he forced a bunch of shit on his kid, and now the kid's a neurotic athlete. Fuck these athletes' relatives. If they wanna be on TV, let 'em get their own goddamn shows. Let 'em go to cable access.

I also don't care if an athlete's wife had a baby, how she is, how the baby is, how much the baby weighs or what the fuckin' baby's name is. It's got nothin' to do with sports. Leave it out!

And I'm tired of athletes whose children are sick. Healthy men with sick children; how banal. The kid's sick? Talk it over privately. Don't spread it all over television. Have some dignity. And play fuckin' ball!!

Nor do I wanna know about some athlete's crippled little brother or his hemophiliac big sister. The Olympics specialize in this kind of mawkish bullshit. Either his aunt has the clap, or his kid has a forty-pound mole, or his high school buddy overdosed on burritos, etc. Can't sports exist on television without all this embarrassing, maudlin, super-sentimental, tear-jerking bullshit? Keep your personal disasters to yourself, and get in there and score some fuckin' points!

And I don't care for all that middlebrow philosophical bullshit you get from athletes and coaches when someone on the team has a serious illness or dies in an accident. They give you that stuff, "When something like this happens, you realize what's really important. It's only a game." Bullshit! If it's only a game, get the fuck out of the business. You know what's important? The score. Who won. I can get plenty of sad tales somewhere else in this victim-packed society. Fuck all that dewy-eyed sentimental bullshit about people who are sick. And that includes any athlete whose father died a week before the game who says, "This one's for Pop." American bathos. Keep it to yourself. Play ball!

And I shouldn't even have to mention severly injured athletes who are playing on "nothing but heart." Fuck you! Suck it up and get out there, motherfucker.

And they're always tellin' ya that one of these athletes has a tumor. Don't they know that no one gives a fuck? You know when you care about a tumor? When *you* have it! Or someone close to you. Who cares about an athlete? No one cares if a rock star gets a tumor. What's so special about an athlete? By the way, you ever notice you don't hear as much about rock stars getting these tumors as you do about athletes? Maybe the drug life is a little better for us than all that stupid sweaty shit the athletes put themselves through. Just speculating.

And I don't wanna know about sports teams that sew the initials of dead people on their jerseys for one whole season as if it really means something. Leave that mawkish bullshit in the locker room. I don't wanna know who's in mourning. Play ball, you fuckin' grotesque overdeveloped nitwits!

And you can skip tellin' me about the Chevrolet player of the game. A thousand-dollar contribution to a scholarship fund in the athlete's name. Shit. A thousand dollars won't even keep a kid in decent drugs for one semester. Fuck Chevrolet.

And when are they gonna discover that no one cares if an athlete is active in local charities? People don't want to know about some coke-headed, steroid monstrosity who's working to help the National Douche Bag Foundation. Or how much he cares about inner-city kids. Can the cocksucker play ball? Fine. Then suit him up and get him the fuck out there on the field and let him injure someone.

One last thing on this topic. No one, repeat, no one is interested in athletes who can sing or play musical instruments. We already have people to perform these tasks. They're called singers and musicians, and, at last count, it would seem we have quite enough of them. The fact that someone with an IQ triple his age has mastered a few simple chords is unimportant and of monumental disinterest. Play ball!

PASS THE ROLES

I'm surprised that all this shit about role models has persisted as long as it has. Why should a kid need a role model? You know what you tell a kid? "Get the fuck out there, get a job, and make a contribution." Never mind that role model shit. If this country is dependent on things like role models, we're much worse off than I thought.

People say athletes should be role models. I never looked up to an athlete, did you? I liked them. I didn't copy them. Did you ever listen to one of those guys talk? Would you want your kid to turn out like that? Willing to completely subordinate his ego and individuality for the sake of a group whose sole purpose is to compete with other groups? Can't have a mustache? Gotta wear a suit jacket? Shit! If your kid needs a role model and you ain't it, you're both fucked.

SPORTS ROUNDUP

I like sports because I enjoy knowing that many of these macho athletes have to vomit before a big game. Any guy who would take a job where you gotta puke first is my kinda guy.

I read that Monica Seles got stabbed. And although I have nothing against Monica Seles, I'm glad somebody in sports got stabbed. I like the idea of it; it's good entertainment. If we're lucky, it'll spread all through sports. And show business, too! Wouldn't you like to see a guy jump up onstage and stab some famous singer? Especially a real shitty pop singer? Maybe they'll even start stabbing comedians. Fuck it, I'm ready! I never perform without my can of mace. I have a switchblade knife, too. I'll cut your eye out and go right on telling jokes.

In football, I root for the Oakland Raiders because they hire castoffs, outlaws, malcontents, and fuckups; they have lots of penalties, fights, and paybacks; and because Al Davis told the rest of the pig NFL owners to go get fucked. Also, they don't have a lot of Christians kneeling down to pray after touchdowns. Christians are ruining sports. Someday, the Raiders will be strong again, and they will dip the ball in shit and shove it down the throats of the wholesome, white, heartland teams that pray together and don't deliver late hits.

You know the best thing I did for myself during the past five years? I told sports to go take a flying fuck. I was fed up with the way I related to professional sports, so I reordered the relationship on my own terms. I became a little more selective.

I couldn't believe how much time I had wasted watching any old piece of shit ballgame that happened to show up on TV. I must have thought there was some inborn male obligation to tune in and root every time a bunch of sweaty assholes got together to mix it up in a stadium somewhere.

I also realized I was wasting perfectly good emotional energy by sticking with my teams when they were doing poorly. My rooting life was scarcely better than those Cubs fans who think it's a sign of character to feel shitty all the time. It's absurd.

I decided it's not necessary to suffer and feel crappy just because my teams suck. What I do now is cut 'em loose for awhile. I simply let them go about losing, as I go about living my life. Then, when they've improved, and are doing well once again, I get back on board and enjoy their success. Yeah, I know, I can hear it: diehard, asshole loyal sports fans screaming, "Front-runner!" Goddamn right! Don't be so fuckin' juvenile. Teams are supposed to provide pleasure and entertainment, not depression and disappointment.

It is also completely unnecessary to suffer several days' emotional devastation just because your team loses some big postseason deal like the Super Bowl. Why on earth would you place your happiness and peace of mind in the hands of several dozen strangers? Listen, folks, if they win, fine; if they lose, fuck 'em! Let 'em practice more. As for you, for Chrissakes find something to do! Get your ass down to the massage parlor and spring for a blow job.

If you really want to enjoy sports, do what I did. Become a Harlem Globetrotters fan. There's no losing, no stats, no strikes, no trades, no contract hassles, no postseason, and no annoying media. Just winning, all the time, every night. By the way, I'm just diseased enough to realize it would also be lots of fun to root for the Washington Generals, the team that loses to the Globetrotters every night. At least you wouldn't have to put up with all that annoying, preseason optimism bullshit.

One common American sports gripe I do not share: I am not like those radio call-in, sports-fan asswipes who think athletes are overpaid. I believe the players should get any amount of money they want, and the fans should go fuck themselves. I'm tired of fans whining all that weak shit about how "we pay their salaries" and "without us there would be no games." Bullshit! Fuck you! If you don't want to spend the money, stay the fuck home! And shut your mouth. Sports fans eat shit.

Sports fans rate even lower than the media and the franchise owners on my scale of miserable, shit-eating vermin. Here's the descending hierarchy: athletes, sports media, team owners, fans. Fans on the bottom. Most sports fans are fat, ignorant, beer-soaked, loudmouth, racist, white male cocksuckers, and they're totally unnecessary to the playing of the games.

The athletes are the only people in sports who count; they're the only ones who are indispensable. Everyone else is superfluous. Think about it. The entire pro-sports sewer began because groups of men got together and played these games in parks, vacant lots, and gyms simply for the fun of it. No money involved; just personal bets. And if today, all the owners, media, and sports fans suddenly disappeared, the athletes would simply go back to the parks, vacant lots, and gyms and play the games by themselves. No one else is necessary.

Of course, if they did, the usual dull people who lack direction would stand around watching, and some businessman-asshole would get the idea of charging admission and giving the players a tiny percentage of the money, and the whole miserable pool of steaming liquid shit would start all over again.

But in spite of all these negative feelings, I still enjoy watching a good close game played by well-matched teams. Lots of scoring, a few good fights, and then preferably forty innings or an octuple overtime, so that both teams eventually run out of players, and many of them are injured because they're tired.

The score of the game is not the only thing I'm interested in. I also root very hard for slumps, losing streaks, penalties, fights, injuries, team dissension, athletes cracking under pressure, and widespread gambling scandals. An earthquake in a ballpark isn't such a bad thing to me, either. I don't give a shit about the outcome of the game, I'm just looking for an interesting story.

I pray that some year the baseball postseason will include only teams with outdoor stadiums in cold-weather cities. And then I hope there are repeated freak storm systems that keep coming through the Midwest and the East, and all during the playoffs there are constant rainouts and postponements. And I pray for the whole thing to continue for months, so the games are pushed further and further back, and eventually the World Series is played in January. And then I hope it's cold and windy and icy and snowy, and a lot of players get hurt, and the games turn out to be a national disgrace. That's the kind of shit I root for.

Then there are other times when I'm not as positive. And I think to myself, Fuck sports! Fuck sweat, fuck jock itch, and fuck all people who are out of breath. Fuck the players, the sports media, the owners, and above all, the sports fans. Double-fuck the sports fans. Actually, though, to tell you the truth, if I had to endure those owners on the same day-to-day basis as I do the sports fans, I'm sure the owners would quickly work their way to the bottom of my list. Lower than a snake's ballbag. Remember, owners are always rotten people no matter what they own, and no matter where they turn up in life.

In their hatred for the players, the fans often forget that the real insects are the owners; the greedy swine owners who are always pleading poverty. In 1980, Nelson Doubleday paid $21.6 million for the Mets franchise. Today it's worth over $200 million. Where's the risk? And if it's so hard to make money in baseball, why are all these maggot entrepreneur-hustlers around the country so eager to pay $95 million for a last-place expansion team?

I'm not too thrilled with the sports media people, either. The talent is marginal, they bring nothing to the mix, and their palpable envy of the players is actually embarrassing. Many of these media stiffs were failed high school and college athletes and simply not good enough to make the cut. (Obviously, I'm excluding former pro ballplayers.) How dare such also-rans criticize athletes and their play? You wanna know the problem? Athletes get tons of money and pussy, and all the best drugs. The sports media don't. Need any more on that?

Some baseball teams hire "ball girls" to retrieve foul balls that don't go into the stands. But I've noticed many of these women are quite feminine and don't throw very well. These teams are making a mistake. I think they should hire lesbians to do that job. Not femmes, but full-on, bad-ass, 90-mile-an-hour bull dykes. The kind you see in hardware stores. I'll tell you one thing, you'd get a lot more good plays and strong return throws out there. And if some fan leaned out of the stands to pick up a foul ball, the "ball dyke" could drag him onto the field and beat the shit out of him for about forty-five minutes.

And if any baseball players tried to stop her, she could just deck them, too.

Athletes like that physical shit. When they're pleased with each other they bump chests, butt heads, and bang forearms. Why don't they just punch each other in the fuckin' teeth? Wouldn't that be great? Teammates, I mean. After a touchdown pass, why doesn't the guy who caught the ball just go over and kick the quarterback right in the nuts? Same with a slam dunk in basketball. The guy who scores oughta grab a chair and beat the living shit out of the guy who fed him the ball. For about forty-five minutes. If this type of celebration were more common, the postgame show from the winners' locker room would be a lot livelier.

And I think there should be at least one sport where the object is to kill someone. A team sport. Deathball. Let's face it, athletes are mostly physical freaks with serious personality defects where competition is concerned, and they just love someone to "motivate" them. Well, what greater motivation can there be than trying to avoid being killed? It's a fuckin' natural! And for me, what could be more fun than watching one of these jackoffs motivate his ugly ass into an early grave every game?

Here's another thing: I love losing streaks. I wish some year a baseball team would lose 162 games. I especially like decades-long, postseason losing streaks. In fact, as soon as my teams are out of the running, I start actively rooting for the Cubs, Red Sox, Bills, Broncos, and Vikings to get as far as they can in the postseason so that ultimately they can let the big prize slip away one more time. I think it is an infinitely more interesting news story for a team to repeatedly fail at the highest level than it is for them to finally win. If the Cubs ever win a World

Series, the news coverage will be the most boring bunch of shit you can imagine.

And, although I wouldn't wish it on anyone, you'll have to admit it would sure be a lot of fun to see a couple of those chartered planes the athletes fly around in go down in flames. I know it might seem ghoulish to the overly squeamish, but I'd love to read about all the hassles they were having restocking the teams, and it would be fun to see the new lineups. Of course, all the stupid shit on TV about the funerals would be real boring.

P.S. Any professional sports team that has a "fight song" is automatically a bush-league, small-town team. Period.

YOU'RE A NATURAL

This is for health food fiends, the natural-fabrics gang, and all those green-head environmental hustlers who stomp around in the "natural": Your key word is meaningless. Everything is natural. Everything in the universe is a part of nature. Polyester, pesticides, oil slicks, and whoopee cushions. Nature is not just trees and flowers. It's everything. Human beings are part of nature. And if a human being invents something, that's part of nature, too. Like the whoopee cushion.

Also: The experience called "natural childbirth" is not natural at all. It is freaky and bizarre. It is distinctly unnatural for a person to invite and welcome pain. Whose influence am I sensing here? Men's? It's nothing more than childbirth machisma. The woman wants it said of her that she can "take it like a man."

LIFE'S LITTLE MOMENTS

- Do you ever look at your watch and immediately forget the time, so you look again? And still it doesn't register, so you have to look a third time. And then someone asks you what time it is, and you actually have to look at your watch for the fourth time in three minutes? Don't you feel stupid?

- Do you ever find yourself standing in a room, and you can't remember why you went in there? And you think to yourself, "Maybe if I go back where I was I'll see something that reminds me. Or maybe it would be quicker if I just stand here and hope it comes back to me." Usually as you're weighing those options, two words float across your mind: "Alzheimer's disease."

- Do you ever have to sneeze while you're taking a piss? It's frightening. Deep down you're afraid you'll release all sorts of bodily fluids into your pants. What people don't realize is that it's physically impossible to sneeze while pissing; your brain won't allow it. Because your brain knows you might blow your asshole out. And wind up having to repaint the entire apartment.

- Have you ever noticed how sometimes all day Wednesday you keep thinking it's Thursday? Then the next day when you're back to normal, you wonder, why don't you think it's Friday?

- Have you ever been sitting on a railroad train in the station, and another train is parked right next to you? And one of them begins moving, but you can't tell which one? And then it becomes obvious, and all the magic is gone? Wouldn't it be nice if we could spend our whole lives not knowing which train was moving? Actually, we do.

- Do you ever fall asleep in the late afternoon and wake up after dark, and for a moment you can't figure out what day it is? You actually find yourself thinking, Could this be yesterday?

- Did you ever tell someone they have a little bit of dirt on their face? They never rub the right spot, do they? They always assume the mirror image and rub the wrong side. Don't you just want to slap the bastard?

- Have you noticed that when your head is on the pillow, if you close one eye the pillow is in one position? But when you switch eyes the pillow seems to move? Sometimes I lie awake for hours doing that.

- Do you ever reach the top of a staircase and think there's one more step? So you take one of those big, awkward steps that doesn't accomplish anything? And then you have to do it a few more times, so people will think it's something you do all the time. "I do this all the time, folks. It's the third stage of syphilis."

EUPHEMISMS: IT'S GETTIN' OLD

Perhaps you've noticed, we no longer have *old people* in this country; they're all gone, replaced by *senior citizens*. Somehow we wound up with millions of these unfortunate creatures known as *golden-agers* and *mature adults*. These are cold, lifeless, antiseptic terms. Typically American. All ways of sidestepping the fear of aging.

And it's not difficult to understand the fear of aging. It's natural. And it's universal; no one wants to get old. No one wants to die. But we do. We die. And we don't like that, so we shade the truth. I started doing it when I reached my forties. I'd look in the mirror at that time and think, "Well, I guess I'm getting . . . *older!*" That sounded a little better than *old*. It sounded like it might even last a bit longer.

But people forget that older is comparative, and they use it as an absolute: "She's an *older woman.*"

"Oh, really? Older than what? Than she used to be? Well, yeah, so?"

People think *getting* old is bad, because they think *being* old is bad. But you know something? Being old is just fine; in fact, it can be terrific. And anyway, it's one of those things you don't get to choose. It's not optional.

But that insufferable group among us known as baby boomers (ages forty-two through fifty-nine, as of 2005) are beginning to get old, and they're having trouble dealing with that. Remember, these baby boomers are the ones who gave us this soft, politically correct language in the first place.

So rather than admit they're getting old, the baby boomers have come up with a new term to describe themselves as they approach the grave. They don't care for *middle-aged*, so instead—get this, folks—instead, they claim to be *pre-elderly*. Don't you love that? Pre-elderly. It's a real word. You don't hear it a lot, but it's out there. The boomers claim that if you're between fifty and sixty-five, you're pre-elderly.

But I'd be willing to bet that in 2011, when they begin turning sixty-five, they will not be calling themselves *elderly*. I have a hunch they'll come up with some new way of avoiding reality, and I have a suggestion for them. They should call themselves the *pre-dead*. It's a perfect term, because, for them, it's accurate and it's highly descriptive.

By the way, those ever-clever boomers have also come up with a word to describe the jobs they feel are most suitable for retired people who wish to keep working. They call these jobs *elder-friendly*. Isn't that sad? God, that's just really, really sad.

And so, to sum up, we have these senior citizens. And, whether I like that phrase or not, unfortunately, I got used to it, and I no longer react too violently when I hear it. But there is still one description for old people that I will never accept. That's when I hear someone describe an old guy as being, for instance, *eighty years young*. Even though I know it's tongue-in-cheek, it makes my skin crawl. It's overly cute and precious, and it's an evasion. It's junk language.

More: On CBS's *60 Minutes*, Lesley Stahl, God help her, actually referred to some old man as being a *ninety-something*. Please. Lesley. I need a small, personal break here.

One last, pathetic example in this category: On the radio, I heard Matt Drudge actually refer to *people of age*. And he

wasn't being sarcastic. He said, "The West Nile virus is a particular threat to people of age." Poor Matt. Apparently, he's
more fucked up than he seems.

Now, going to an adjacent subject: One unfortunate fact
of life for many of these eighty- or ninety-somethings is that
they're forced to live in places where they'd rather not be. Old-
people's homes. So what name should we use for these places
where we hide our old people? When I was a little boy, there
was a building in my neighborhood called the *home for the aged*.
It had a copper sign on the gate: HOME FOR THE AGED. It
always looked deserted; I never saw anyone go in. Naturally, I
never saw anyone come out, either.

Later, I noticed people started calling those places *nursing
homes* and *rest homes*. Apparently, it was decided that some of
these old people needed nurses, while others just needed a
little rest. What you hear them called now is *retirement homes*
or *long-term-care facilities*. There's another one of those truly
bloodless terms: long-term-care facility.

But actually, it makes sense to give it a name like that,
because if you do, you make it a lot easier for the person
you're putting in there to acquiesce and cooperate with you.
I remember old people used to tell their families, "Whatever
you do, don't put me in a home. Please don't put me in a
home." But it's hard to imagine one of them saying, "Whatever
you do, don't put me in a long-term-care facility." So calling
it that is really a trick. "C'mon, Grandpa, it's not a home. It's
long-term care!"

By the way, while we're on the subject of the language of
getting old, I want to tell you something that happened to me
in New York on a recent evening. I was standing in line at the
Carnegie Deli to pay my check, and there was a guy ahead of
me who looked like he was in his sixties. He gave the cashier
a ten-dollar bill, but apparently, it wasn't enough. When the

cashier mentioned it to him in a nice way, he said, "Oh, I'm sorry. I guess I had a *senior moment*." And I thought how sad that was. To blame a simple mistake on the fact that you're in your sixties, even if you're just sort of joking. As if anyone would think a twenty-year-old couldn't make the same mistake. I only mention this because it's an example of how people can brainwash themselves by adopting popular language.

I wanted to pull him aside and say, "Listen, I just heard you refer to yourself as a senior. And I wanted to ask, were you by any chance a junior last year? Because if you weren't a junior last year, then you're not a senior *this* year." I wanted to say it, but I figured, why would he listen to me? After all, I'm only a freshman.

FUNERALS

I don't like to attend funerals. When I die, I don't want a funeral, because I'm sure of one thing: if I don't like other people's funerals, I'm going to hate my own.

And I don't want a wake. I don't like the idea of lying on display, dead, in a mahogany convertible with the top down. Everybody looking, and you're dead. They have no idea you're wearing short pants, and have no back in your jacket. It's embarrassing. Especially if they use too much makeup, and you look like a deceased drag queen.

And as you're lying there half-naked, one by one they kneel down and stare silently into your coffin. It's supposed to look reverent. What they're really doing is subtracting their age from yours to find out how much time they have left. That is, if they're younger. If they're older, they just gloat because you died first.

"He looks good."

"Dave, he's dead."

"I know. But when he was alive he didn't look this good."

It's a perverse fact that in death you grow more popular. As soon as you're out of everyone's way, your approval curve moves sharply upward. You get more flowers when you die than you got your whole life. All your flowers arrive at once. Too late.

And people say the nicest things about you. They'll even make things up: "You know, Jeff was a scumbag. A complete degenerate scumbag. But he meant well! You have to give him that. He was a complete degenerate well-meaning scumbag. Poor Jeff."

"Poor" is a big word when discussing the dead.

"Poor Bill is dead."

"Yeah, poor Bill."

"And poor Tom is gone."

"Jeez, yeah, poor Tom."

"Poor John died."

"Poor John. Hey, what about Ed?"

"Ed? That motherfucker is still alive! I wish he would die."

"Yeah. The dirty prick. Let's kill him."

SEVEN DEATH WISHES

1. You're in a leather bar with 200 heavily armed, wildly drunk, ex-convict, sadomasochistic butch lesbians. You climb on the bar and say, "Which one of you sweet little cupcakes wants the privilege of being the first in line to suck me off? If you're the lucky one, and you give me a real good blow job, I might do you a favor and throw you a quick fuck and let you cook me a nice meal. C'mon, line up, you repulsive cunts, and I'll change your sexual orientations. I dare you to cut off my balls!"

2. Walking through the woods one day, you encounter a group of devil worshipers who are disemboweling a small boy. You tell them what they're doing is cowardly, unnatural, and morally wrong, and you're sure they would never try it on a grown-up. Especially one like yourself, who loves Jesus, and always wears his crucifix proudly. You also say that you just arrived from Australia, have no local friends or living relatives, and are planning to establish a Christian church called Fuck Lucifer. Then you order them to stay where they are, because you're leaving to get the police.

3. You and your wife are the only nonbikers at a Hell's Angels' wedding, where all the others have been drinking, shooting methamphetamine, and smoking PCP for eleven straight days. At the height of the celebration, you whip out your dick, grab the bride's crotch, and shout to the crowd, "I understand you filthy, greasy asshole motorcycle cowards are supposed to be real good at gang rape, but I'll bet you can't fuck like me! Watch this!" You begin ripping the wedding gown off the bride, pointing out that your own wife is a virgin, and that you, yourself, have never been fucked in the ass.

4. At a white supremacists' convention in remote Idaho, you take the stage wearing an ATF helmet and a Malcolm X T-shirt, and holding a United Nations flag. You perform a rap song that says morally and intellectually inferior white people should submit themselves to black rule and turn over their wives and daughters to black men as a way of apologizing for slavery. You mention that following your recent conversion to Judaism, you have become ashamed of your white skin and would gladly have it removed if you could just find a way to do it.

5. Three sadistic sex maniacs have entered your house, and they find you naked in the shower. The most coherent among them asks if he can play with your genitals. You lose your temper and say, "Listen, you perverted, lunatic fuck, leave my sex organs alone. And tell your drooling, fruitcake buddies I would rather place my cock in that paper shredder located by the window, or stuff my testicles into the

Cuisinart, which is in the kitchen on the right-hand shelf, than let you disgusting degenerates touch my private parts."

6. While attending the First Communion of a Mafia boss's grandson, you suddenly begin to pistol-whip the boy's mother, screaming, "I'm gonna hit you some more, you ugly dago bitch, and if one of these greasy, dickless criminal morons who call themselves men makes a move on me, I'll break his guinea neck. I'm hungry! Make me some fuckin' spaghetti and go easy on the oil, ya hairy greaseball cunt!"

7. You're standing in a crowded Harlem bar dressed in the robes of a Ku Klux Klan Grand Dragon, holding a Confederate flag, and singing "Dixie" in a real loud voice with a Mississippi accent. You jump on the bar, shit in the drink of a huge man with numerous razor scars on his face, wipe your ass with a picture of Martin Luther King, and yell at the man, "Hey, boy! Get your momma down here, I want some dark meat. And get that fuckin' jungle-bunny music off the juke box, or I'm gonna start killin' me some boogies!"

Have a nice afterlife.

SUICIDE: THE OPTION

Part 1: An Introductory Course

The Time Is Ripe

Do you realize that right now—right this second—somewhere around the world some guy is gettin' ready to kill himself? Isn't that great? Do you ever stop to think about that kinda shit? I do. It's interesting. It's fun. And it's true! Think about it: Right this second, some guy is gettin' ready to bite the big bazooka! Because statistics show that every year a million people commit suicide. A million! That's 2,800 a day. That's one every thirty seconds. Think about it: Since you've been reading this, another guy has bit the dust.

It's a Guy Thing

And I say "guy," because men are four times more likely than women to commit suicide—even though women attempt it more. So men are better at it! That's something else you gals'll wanna be workin' on. If you want to be truly equal, you're going to have to start takin' your own lives in greater numbers.

But personally, I just think it's interesting to know that at any moment the odds are good . . . that some guy is draggin' a chair across the garage floor . . . tryin' to get it right underneath that ceiling beam. Wouldn't want to be too far off center. If it's worth doin', it's worth doin' right.

Somewhere else, another guy is goin' over and gettin' a gun out of a dresser drawer. Somebody else is opening up a brand-new package of razor blades—maybe struggling with the packaging a little bit.

"Goddamn plastic! Why do they wrap these things so fuckin' tight? Shit! It's always some fuckin' thing. Nothing ever goes right! Goddamn fuckin' shit prick!"

I just think suicide is interesting as hell. It's probably the most interesting thing you can do with your life. End it!

Part 2: All Suicide, All the Time

It Sure Beats Golf

Suicide is an interesting topic, because it's an inherently interesting decision: to decide voluntarily not to exist anymore. It's profound. You know what it is? It's the ULTIMATE MAKEOVER. That's why I think it belongs on television. In this depraved culture? With the shit that passes for entertainment in this country? Suicide would be a natural on television. People would love it. In fact, I'll bet you could have an all-suicide channel. On cable TV. I'll bet. Shit, they've got all-golf. What the fuck? You ever watch golf? It's like watching flies fuck.

If you can get a bunch of brainless, white male assholes to sit still and waste a Sunday afternoon watchin' that kinda bullshit, you *know* you can get some people to watch suicides. All day long. Twenty-four hours a day, nothing but suicide. Must-die TV!

C'mon Down!

You'd get a lot of people watching that kinda shit; you'd get a lot of people volunteering to be *on* there, too. Just so their friends could see them on TV. People are goofy. You'd get a *lot* of volunteers. You'd get all those leftover assholes from *Let's Make a Deal*. They'd be lined up around the block, pushing each other out of the way, putting on funny capes and hats and makeup and calling themselves "Captain Suicide!"

People would be competing for Most Unusual Method: They'd be jumpin' off of barns, lightin' themselves on fire, puttin' rat poison on a taco, drinking Mop & Glo, sticking mothballs up their ass. You'd probably have some weird fuck show up who figured out how to kill himself with a Stinger missile and some dental floss. People are fuckin' goofy!

I'll bet you could find a married couple—in one of them trailer parks or somethin'?—who'd be perfectly willing—perfectly willing!—to sit in a loveseat and blow each other's heads off with shotguns. While a love song is playin'. People are fuckin' nuts!

E Pluribus Unum

This country is full of nitwits and assholes. You ever notice that? Nitwits, assholes, fuckups, scumbags, jerk-offs, and dip-shits. And they all vote!

In fact, sometimes you get the impression they're the *only* ones who vote. You can usually tell who's been doin' the voting by lookin' at the election returns. It sure ain't me out there, wastin' my time with a meaningless activity like that.

You know those people on *The Jerry Springer Show*? Those are the average Americans. Oh, yeah, believe me. The below average can't get on the show. The below average are all sittin' home, watchin' that shit on TV. Gettin' ready to go out and vote. Fillin' out their sample ballot.

Dumb-De-Dumb-Dumb

Americans are dumb. AMERICANS ARE FUCKIN' DUMB!

You can say what you want about this country—and I love it here; I wouldn't live anywhere else:

- I love the freedoms we used to have.
- I loved when it didn't take a natural disaster for us to care for one another longer than five minutes at a time.
- I loved when we weren't on camera all day long, indoors and out, from every conceivable angle.

So, I love this country. I wouldn't live any other place at any other time in history. BUT! BUT! Say what you want about America—Land of the Free, Home of the Brave—we've got some dumb-ass motherfuckers floatin' around this country. Dumb-ass motherfuckers.

Now, of course, that's just my opinion; you can think what you want about the American people. You can think of them as smart, dumb, naïve, innocent, ignorant, gullible, easily led, blissfully unaware—whatever you like . . .

Part 3: The Pyramid

The Ratings Game

But no matter what you think of the American people, you're gonna have to deal with them, because you're in the television business now. You've got the All-Suicide Channel on cable TV;

you need viewers. You have to worry about ratings; you have to worry about . . . sweeps months!

By now, most folks know what sweeps months are—the most important ratings months of the year. When the networks put on all their biggest attractions and hottest stars, trying to pump up the ratings, so their local stations can adjust their advertising rates. So, you're going to have to deal with that competitive television-industry mentality; you're going to have to get out there and compete for viewers.

So I think, during sweeps months . . . on the All-Suicide Channel . . . you're gonna have to go with mass suicides. Huge, public events, on live television, where hundreds of people kill themselves all at the same time.

Sounds Like a Plan

Now, the question is: How are you going to do this? How are you going to get large numbers of people to commit suicide all at once, at a time and place of your choosing? In fact, how are you going to get people to commit suicide in the first place? Where will these people come from?

In order to make this whole thing work, you'll need careful planning and organization. You're gonna need a system; you can't just sit around all day, waiting for people to drop by the studio and commit suicide. You need a plan. And folks, today must be your lucky day, because, as it happens, I have just such a plan. Here's what we do:

Pyramid Scheme

The first thing we need is to build up a large pool of suicide volunteers—people who can be easily persuaded to kill themselves. Essentially, what we're looking for are people without hope: individuals society has given up on, fate has given up on, or who have completely given up on themselves. Rock-bottom, dead-end, totally fucked-up people with no hope, no future, and no reason to live. A pool of the hopeless, to serve as suicide volunteers. Think of it as a pyramid. That gives us a visual fix. The Pyramid of the Hopeless. So let's get busy and build our Pyramid.

Bottoming Out

Naturally, we have to start at the bottom, and in this lowest layer, I think we oughta put the homeless people. God knows, we've got enough of them. In fact, we've got so many, we don't know how many there are. Nobody gives a fuck about 'em, nobody wants 'em, nobody's got a plan, nobody's got a program, nobody's got any money. Society doesn't give a fuck about homeless people. They're totally hopeless, so, in the Pyramid they go.

Pen Pals

The next group we're gonna deal with is these people in prison. Especially the ones serving extremely long sentences. And I'll grant you, many of the sentences are deserved. I'm sure as many as half the people in prison are in there for things they really did. And that's not a bad average, one out of two.

But this is obviously another group that nobody gives a shit about. We don't rehabilitate them, because we say rehabilitation doesn't work. And it probably doesn't work because if they do get out of prison, nobody will give 'em a job, anyway. So they're in a hopeless loop of crime and punishment.

And the judges give 'em these extreme, draconian sentences. They get 60-, 70-, 80-, 100-year sentences; life terms,

double life terms. One guy recently—and I swear this is true—
one guy was given three consecutive life terms—plus two
death penalties. Well, how the fuck do you serve that? Even
David Copperfield can't do that. You gotta be a Hindu to pull
that shit off. Then you've got the people on death row, a couple
thousand of them. They ain't goin' anywhere. Boom! In the
fuckin' Pyramid they go.

Another Crappy Day

Now, this next group going into our Pyramid is, more or less,
self-selected—and possibly a bit controversial to some folks.
These are these people who claim to be depressed. Apparently,
in this land of plenty, the richest nation in the history of the
world (we're so proud of saying that), where some of our super-
markets have over a hundred thousand items on their shelves,
we have 19 million Americans who claim to be depressed. And
some of them take medicine for it. And, sometimes, the medicine makes them commit suicide, which *really* depresses the shit
out of the rest of them. No hope for these folks—in they go!

And let's not forget the ones who only *think* they're
depressed. They *think* they're depressed, because they saw the
Prozac commercial on television and the doctor looked like a
nice guy, the music sounded kind of peppy, and, ". . . what the
fuck, some of these pills might just pick me right up." Hopeless
mind-set. In the fuckin' Pyramid. Quickly!

Choose Your Disease Carefully

Now we come to the top of our magnificent structure of despair,
and this ultimate space has been reserved for those who are
truly sick: the terminally ill. No pretenders here. Hundreds of
thousands of dead-enders with no hope at all:

- Some of them have something there's no cure for.

- Some of them have something there's no cure for, and nobody's lookin' for a cure, because there ain't enough people sick with what they got, so there ain't no money in the cure.

- Some of them have something there's a cure for, but they haven't got the money for the cure.

- Some of them have something there's a cure for, they've got the money, but they're too far gone.

- Some of them have something there's a cure for, they've got the money, they're not too far gone, but they don't have a ride. And most of those people are too sick to commit suicide. BOOM! In the Pyramid.

Taking Stock

Now, let's review and see what we have. Let's put ourselves in the office of vice president of programming at the All-Suicide Channel and analyze what there is to work with. Well, thanks to our carefully thought-out Pyramid of the Hopeless, we find ourselves blessed with an abundance of homeless, imprisoned, condemned, depressed, and terminally ill people—probably millions of them. In other words, we've hit the jackpot. And let's not forget, many of these people more than likely fall into several categories.

Jumping to Conclusions

So, here's my idea, as well as the premise it's based on: I'm convinced that in this depraved culture that so devalues human life and dignity, and where reality television has convinced everyone they belong on national TV, I'm convinced that if you added in the excitement of a brand-new All-Suicide Channel debuting with maximum publicity, you could get five hundred of these hopeless people to hold hands and jump into the Grand Canyon. I'll fuckin' bet you. I'll bet you you could get that done in this country right now.

I'm convinced they would do it. For money! Oh, for money! You gotta give 'em *some*thing. You gotta make it worth their while. After all, they're Americans—they're for sale. Give 'em a little something. Give them a toaster. Americans will do anything, but you gotta give 'em a toaster, don't you?

Eyes on the Prize

So give 'em a little prize—everybody wants a prize. Give 'em some sorta gizmo. Give 'em a cell phone—give 'em a laptop. Give 'em a cell phone that takes a *picture* of a laptop. Give 'em a laptop that takes a picture of a cell phone!

Give 'em an all-terrain vehicle; give 'em a riding lawn mower, a snowblower, an outdoor barbecue, a Jet Ski. In other words, give 'em one of those things they buy for themselves when they're tryin' to take their minds off how badly they're gettin' fucked by the system.

Here's an idea: Just before they jump into the canyon, give 'em a hat with a built-in camera; tell 'em it's a Jump-Cam. Tell 'em you'll send the video home to the family. How about a T-shirt? Who don't want a T-shirt? Nobody! Give 'em a nice T-shirt:

"I COMMITTED SUICIDE, AND ALL I GOT WAS THIS STUPID FUCKIN' SHIRT."

Leap of Faith

And how about this: If you *really* want to raise the profile of this promotion—if you really want to attract attention—get a bunch of those evangelical Christians to participate and call it "Jump for Jesus!" They'd go for it in a minute. "Jump for Jesus!"

But let's be fair about these Christians, because they do come in for a lot of abuse these days. So let's be fair: All Christians really want out of life is to die—and go see Jesus. So, give them a helping hand. Be a Good Samaritan, and do the Christian thing. Get 'em to jump in the canyon.

Tell 'em it's a shortcut to heaven. Mention the word *martyr*. It works with the Moslems, it works with the Catholics; who knows? It might even work with these folks. You never know.

Give them a little encouragement. "He's down there. He's at the bottom of the canyon. Look for the man with the glowing head."

Part 4: Ah, Youth

Networking

You could have a lot of fun with a channel like that. A *lotta* fun. But you know somethin'? You might not want to be on cable. Cable has a limited audience. You might want to get more people lookin' in, and, if so, you're gonna have to go to the broadcast networks; one of the big broadcast networks. Now, I don't know about you, but when I think about suicide and network television, I'm thinkin' FOX! I'm tellin' you, if the people at FOX ain't sittin' around having meetings on an idea like this, they ain't doin' their goddamn jobs over there.

So you put this thing on FOX—and you get Budweiser to sponsor it. Well, Budweiser and a whole bunch of car companies, so people can be thinkin' about drinkin' and drivin' at the same time. Isn't that fun? Isn't it fun to watch the commercials they run during sporting events on TV? "Drink this! Drive that! Fuck you!" They don't care. They don't give a shit about you. And then every now and then they qualify their message. "Don't let your friends drive drunk." Yeah, sure.

Get 'em While They're Young

So you put this thing on FOX. And if you do—or if you put it on any broadcast network—you're gonna have to bring in a younger audience. Everybody knows, that's what the advertisers are looking for: eighteen- to twenty-four-year-olds. So you'll have to get young people interested in this, and you know how you do that? You know how you get young people interested in suicide? You don't call it suicide. You call it EXTREME LIVING! They'd eat it up.

Let's face it, young people are attracted to suicide in the first place. Did you know suicide is the third-leading cause of death between fifteen and twenty-four? It's third! It's ninth in the general population. That'll give you an idea of how popular this after-school activity has become . . . among our teenage folks.

Boy's Life

Especially these young boys, these adolescent males. And a lot of them, you know, they kill themselves when they're jerking off. Yeah. They don't mean to. It just happens. You know about that? Jerkin' off and dyin'? Most people never heard of it. It's just one of those things Americans can't handle, so nobody talks about it. It's not on *Larry King Live*, it's not on Barbara Walters, and you're not gonna see it in *People* magazine. But it's out there, folks. And it's extremely common.

You just ask any teenage boy what he knows or what he's heard . . . about cuttin' off your air supply just at the moment you're about to have a sexual release. He'll tell you an interesting story or two. The kids call it scarfing, because some of them use scarves to do it.

Do It Yourself

Or screw the kid, you don't need him. Just get on the Internet and Google in the words *autoerotic asphyxia*. It's the practice of cutting off the oxygen to the brain at the last moment during masturbation, in order to heighten and intensify the orgasm. And when I say common? A thousand kids a year die from this. A thousand of 'em, okay? So if that many kids die, think how many of 'em are tryin' to pull this off. If you'll pardon the pun I threw in there just to lighten the mood.

The Way Things Work

But here's the way it works—apparently. Apparently! I mean, I never tried it; it sounded kinda risky to me. Jerkin' off is all I need, you know what I mean? I ain't tryin' to double my money; fuck that shit. Not me. I just jerk off, wipe off my chest, get up, and go to work. Nothin' fancy. Nothin' fancy at our house, we're simple folk.

But here's the way it's *supposed* to work—and this is why it's such a big attraction in the first place: Apparently, it is true, physiologically speaking, that if you cut off your air supply—the oxygen to your brain—just at the moment you're about to have an orgasm, the orgasm is about . . . I don't know, let's say five hundred times better. Somethin' like that—it's incredibly intense. So what you've gotta do is stand up on a chair, or a bucket or something like that, and you put a rope around your neck, and you start jerkin' off.

And while you're pullin' your pud—while you're whalin' away—you have to arrange to almost strangle yourself . . . just before you have an orgasm. And by the way, while all this activity is goin' on, you've gotta maintain a hard-on. Which ain't easy, 'cause you might just be gettin' ready to buy the farm. So you better be fantasizin' about somebody you really like . . . or some*thing* you really like . . . I don't know what it might be. Maybe gettin' fucked in the ass by a game warden, who knows? Hey, I'm not here to judge. We're all different. To each his own.

So let's recap: Standin' on a chair, rope around your neck, peter in your hand. Now you have to time it just right, so that just before you come—you almost die! And sometimes you miscalculate. You don't know if you're comin' or goin'.

Blame Game

And the parents of these kids are too embarrassed to tell the police, so they put the kid's dick away and say he had poor grades. Or, "His girlfriend left him." "Well, no wonder, lady. Look at his fuckin' hobbies." And the policeman writes it down as suicide, once again screwing up the statistics.

Then they blame the whole thing on heavy metal music. You know about that? Ever since the incident with Judas Priest about twenty years ago, they blame suicide on heavy metal. If you remember, Judas Priest is a heavy metal band, and in 1985, two kids in Nevada spent all day listening to one of their albums and then they killed themselves. And ever since that time, heavy metal gets blamed for teenage suicide. If it's murder, they tend to blame rap.

Don't Look at Us

But it's never the parents. You ever notice that?

Apparently—if you listen to them—parents bear no responsibility for turnin' out a fucked-up kid; or even a good kid who *gets* fucked up. Parents have to be the most full-of-shit people in the world. Always have been. Top to bottom, front to back—completely full of shit.

But it comes with the job, doesn't it? In fairness, it's really part of the job description. If you want to be a parent, you've gotta be full of shit. At least half the time.

When you think about it; parents have it both ways. If the kid turns out to be a loser, they had nothin' to do with that. "Must be those kids he hangs around with down at the parking lot." But boy, if he's a winner? Got a scholarship or somethin' like that? Man, they're the first ones out there, raisin' their hands, tryin' to take a little credit. It's a nice state of mind . . . if you can talk yourself into believin' it.

PEOPLE WHO
SHOULD BE PHASED OUT

- Guys who always harmonize the last few notes of "Happy Birthday."
- People over 40 who can't put on reading glasses without making self-conscious remarks about their advancing age.
- Guys who wink when they're kidding.
- Men who propose marriage on the giant TV screen at a sports stadium.
- Guys in their fifties who flash me the peace sign and really mean it.
- People with a small patch of natural white hair who think it makes them look interesting.
- Guys with creases in their jeans.
- People who know a lot of prayers by heart.
- People who move their lips—when *I'm* talking!
- Guys who want to shake my hand even though we just saw each other an hour ago.

- A celebrity couple who adopt a Third-World baby and call it Rain Forest.

- Guys who wear suits all day and think an earring makes them cool at night.

- Old people who tell me what the weather used to be where they used to live.

- Men who have one long, uninterrupted eyebrow.

- Guys who wink and give me the peace sign simultaneously.

- People who say, "Knock knock," when entering a room and, "Beep beep," when someone is in their path.

- Fat guys who laugh at everything.

- People who have memorized a lot of TV-show theme songs and are really proud of it.

- Women who think it's cute to have first names consisting solely of initials.

- People who give their house or car a name.

- People who give their genitals a name.

- Guys who can juggle, but only a little bit.

- Actors who drive race cars.

- Men who wear loafers without socks. Especially if they have creases in their jeans.

- Athletes and coaches who give more than a hundred percent.

- Guys who still smell like their soap in the late afternoon.

- Blind people who don't want any help.

- Guys who wear their watches on the inside of their wrists.

- Any man who wears a suit and tie to a ballgame.

- Guys who flash me the thumbs-up sign. Especially if they're winking and making the peace sign with the other hand.

EUPHEMISMS:
BROKE, NUTS, AND ON THE STREET

I Got No Money

While we in America have been busy creating politically correct euphemisms for old people—thereby making their lives infinitely easier—we've also been working on our poor-people language problem. And we now have language that takes all the pain out of being poor. Having no money these days is easier than ever.

I can remember, when I was young, that *poor people lived in slums*. Not anymore. These days, the *economically disadvantaged occupy substandard housing in the inner cities*. It's so much nicer for them. And yet they're still considered *socially marginal*.

But as it turns out, many of these socially marginal people receive *public assistance*—once known as *welfare*. Before that it was called *being on relief*, or *being on the dole*. And at that time, being on the dole was the worst thing you could say about a family: "They're on the dole." People were ashamed. It was tough to get a date if you were on the dole.

But public assistance! That sounds good. Who of us hasn't benefited from some form of public assistance? Even huge businesses and agricultural interests receive public assistance.

Ditto all the wealthiest taxpayers. So apparently, there is no shame attached to being on the dole after all.

I Got No Home

In this country, about the only thing worse than having no money is having no place to live. And over the years, those with no place to live have had many different names: *vagrants, tramps, hoboes, drifters,* and *transients* come to mind. Which name applied to a person sometimes depended on his, his—God, this is difficult to say—*lifestyle*. There, it's out.

But can having no place to live actually be a lifestyle? Well, it seems to me that if you're going to use a questionable word like *lifestyle* at all, you should be forced to use it across the board. After all, if there's a *gay lifestyle*—which I doubt—and a *suburban lifestyle*—which seems more arguable—it stands to reason there must be a *homeless lifestyle*. And even, one would assume, a *prison lifestyle*.

Indeed, is it possible that those doomed souls in places like Buchenwald were actually enjoying a *concentration-camp lifestyle*? If they were, don't tell their families; you'll be misunderstood. And, taking this unfortunate word to its ultimate, logical extreme, I will not be surprised to someday see one of those spiritual mediums doing a TV show called *Lifestyles of the Dead*. (Incidentally, shouldn't a group of mediums be called *media*? Just asking.)

Back to the subject: vagrants, tramps, hoboes, drifters, and transients. Without using a dictionary (which in many cases is no help at all), here are the distinctions I picked up in years past by listening to how people used these words. The sense I got was: Vagrants simply had no money; tramps and hoboes had no money, but they moved around; drifters moved around, but occasionally worked for a while and then drifted on, whereas tramps and hoboes didn't work at all. We'll get to transients in a moment.

There's one other distinction between tramps and hoboes that's worth mentioning. The word *tramp* might also have been used to describe the young woman your son brought home. Rarely did anyone's son bring home a hobo. Unless, of course, he was into the *gay hobo lifestyle*. Actually, there weren't too many gay hoboes. That's because if a hobo didn't have a home, he certainly didn't have a closet either to be in or to come out of. (Sudden thought: hobo rhymes with homo. Sorry.)

Another way to categorize this class of people was to call them transients. Sometimes, on skid row, where they had a lot of *bums* and *winos* (we'll get to them in a minute), you'd see a cheap hotel with a sign that said TRANSIENTS WELCOME.

Transients were like drifters, except transients seemed to stay in cities, whereas drifters moved through small towns and rural areas. You *had* to move through those places, because they weren't as tolerant as cities; they didn't have signs that said DRIFTERS WELCOME. It was usually just the opposite. Ask Clint Eastwood. By the way, isn't a hotel that says it welcomes transients a little like a restaurant that says it prefers people with stomachs? Just asking.

First cousin to a *transient hotel* was a *flophouse*, a magnificently descriptive piece of language that has all but disappeared. (Just for the record, these days transient hotels are called *limited service lodgings*.) Several cuts above all these places were *furnished rooms*, these days known by the phrase *SROs*, short for *single room occupancy*.

So, staying on track here, we began this section with people who have no place to live, which brings us to today's hot designation, *the homeless*, also known as *street people*. When I was a boy, we never heard those words; a dirty, drunk man on the street who wanted money was normally called a bum. Simple word, three letters, one syllable: *bum*. And a bum was usually also a wino. You know, a *substance abuser*. He had a *chemical dependency*. Little did we know.

By the way, it should be pointed out that *bum* might also have been used to describe the young man your daughter brought home. Many's the bum who didn't pass muster with Dad. I wonder how many of those bums the daughters brought home wound up marrying the tramps the sons brought home? That might explain all those *homeless children*.

But the word *homeless* is useless. It's messy, it's inaccurate, it's not descriptive. It attempts to cover too many things: poverty, alcoholism, drug addiction, schizophrenia, no place to live, and begging on the street.

Homeless should mean only one thing: no home. No place to live. Many of these people who beg on the street actually have places to live. I had one guy tell me he needed money to buy tires for his van. I gave him a dollar; I considered him both honest and enterprising.

The first word I remember for these people was *bag ladies*. I don't know why men were left out of this; I never heard anyone say *bag men*. I guess that's because a bag man is a different thing. A bag man is someone who delivers bribes or illegal gambling money. Probably, in today's evasive, dishonest, politically correct language, they'd be called *bag persons*. In my opinion, the closest we're ever going to get to a good descriptive name for these lovable grimy folks is street people.

And by the way, isn't it ironic that shopping bags (and shopping carts)—symbols of plenty—should be the objects most preferred by people who have nothing at all? I guess if you have nothing, you need something to carry it around in. Especially if you're crazy.

Wild and Crazy Guys

That's what a lot of these street people are, you know. They're crazy. I avoid terms like *mentally disturbed* and *emotionally impaired*. You can't let the politically correct language police dictate the way you express yourself. I prefer plain language: crazy, insane, nuts. "The whole world is crazy, and many of its inhabitants are insane. Or am I just nuts?" And for the most part, we humans do enjoy being colorful and creative when describing the condition of someone who's crazy. Here are a few descriptions of craziness that I enjoy:

- One wheel in the sand.
- Seat back not in the full, upright position.
- Not playing with a full bag of jacks.
- Doesn't have both feet in the end zone.
- Lives out where the buses don't run.
- The cheese fell off his cracker a long time ago.
- His factory's still open, but it's makin' something else.

Here's an odd one: *His squeegee doesn't go all the way to the bottom of the pail.* I think you have to have some serious time-management problems to be sitting around thinking up stuff like that. But there you are. This next one sounds really good, but I confess I don't quite understand it: *He belongs in a cotton box.* For some reason it sounds exactly right, though, doesn't it?

And if you're going to be irreverent about describing crazy people, you can't get soft when it comes to describing the places we keep them. Or used to keep them. In the 1980s, Ronald Reagan decided the best place to keep them was on the streets, which actually makes a lot of sense, because the streets are nothing more than a slightly larger, open-air asylum, anyway.

But around the turn of the nineteenth century, many states had places called *institutions for the feebleminded.* That name seemed too long for some people, so instead they referred to them as *madhouses.* "They took him to the madhouse. Boy, was he mad." Then these places became *insane asylums, mental homes, mental institutions,* and finally, *psychiatric facilities.*

I have three personal favorites. I always liked the *hoo-hoo hotel.* To me, that says it all. Here's another one that's not bad: *the puzzle factory.* It has a certain class to it, doesn't it? But if you prefer a gentler approach, you really can't beat *the enchanted kingdom.* "They took him away to the enchanted kingdom." And guess how they took him there? The *twinkymobile.* Now that's descriptive language.

TERRORISM MISNOMERS

Domestic Terrorism

When they talk about domestic terrorism, they often cite the Oklahoma City bombing. But that wasn't terrorism. Terrorism involves a series of acts intended to put a civilian population in a state of panic, fear, and uncertainty, in order to achieve some political goal. Oklahoma City wasn't terrorism, it was payback. Revenge. Timothy McVeigh wanted to punish the federal government for what it did at Waco and Ruby Ridge. Revenge, not terrorism.

Terrorism Expert

Television news channels will often present some guest they identify as a *terrorism expert*. But you can take one look at him and see that he's clearly not a terrorism expert. He's a guy in a suit who obviously works in an office. And I say he's not a terrorism expert.

You wanna know who's a terrorism expert? Osama bin Laden. Ayman al-Zawahiri. The people they hang around with. Those are the terrorism experts. Has this guy in the suit ever blown anyone up? No. So why is he a terrorism expert?

I'm sure the TV people would say, "Well, because he's made a study of terrorism." Oh, I see. So really, he's an expert in the study of terrorism, the subject of terrorism. But can he make a suicide vest? Fuck, no. And if he can, he should make one, put it on, and press the button. Then he'll be a real terrorism expert. Like those people he now only reads about.

Suicide Bomber

No. Sorry to disagree; it's anything *but* suicide. A person who commits suicide is someone who places no value on his life: "My life is worthless, I'm going to end it." These so-called suicide bombers don't feel that way. They feel their lives are worth something, and that by giving them up they make a statement to the world, furthering a cause they believe in deeply. In their eyes, their lives (when sacrificed) have value. And, by the way, the "suicide bombers" themselves don't call it that. In a stunning example of euphemism, they call it a *sacred explosion*. Holy smoke!

"Homicide Bombers"

And in spite of what Bush has been ordered to say, they're not *homicide bombers*, either. All bombings are intended to kill people, to produce homicides. Anyone who packs a bomb with nails and bits of steel, and sets it off in a public place, is hoping to commit homicide. This is true of any bomb, whether you drop it out of an airplane or leave it on a doorstep; you're hoping to kill people. That's the purpose. Killing people. In the case of these so-called suicide bombs, what's different is that the people setting them off are intentionally ending their own lives in the process. That's why we confuse the act with suicide.

Human Shields

During bombing raids in Iraq, the media liked to say that
Saddam Hussein used people as *human shields*. That's not accurate. Although it's true they were used as shields, the fact is
they were humans already. So if these humans were used as
shields, they *were* human shields. They weren't *being used as*
human shields.

Got that?

Cowards

Bush calls the al-Qaeda people cowards, and says, "They like
to hide." Well, isn't that what the American Continental Army
did during the American Revolution? Our beloved patriots?
They hid. They hid behind trees. Then they came out, killed
some British soldiers, and ran away. Just like al-Qaeda. That's
what you do when you're outnumbered and have less fire-
power than the enemy. It's called "trying to win." It's not
cowardly.

Bill Maher may have stretched the point a bit when he said
that air force pilots who release their bombs from hundreds
of miles away are cowards; flying combat jets doesn't attract
many cowards. But it's not nearly as courageous an act as
deliberately strapping a bomb to your chest and heading for
the disco with no intention of dancing.

I will say this. Getting out of the Vietnam War through
Daddy's connections and then not living up to your end of the
bargain is probably a form of cowardice.

"Heroes" Who "Died for Their Country"

The Port Authority of New York and New Jersey said that changing the name of Newark Airport to Liberty International Airport would be a way of honoring "the more than 3,000 heroes who died for their country in the World Trade Center." Pardon me for pointing this out, folks, but stock traders, clerks, receptionists, cooks, waiters, and building maintenance people in the World Trade Center didn't *die for their country*. They died because they went to work. Not one of them would have shown up for work that day if you had told them they would die as a result. Try to get your heroes straight.

Not everyone who died in 9/11 was a *hero*. *Hero* is a very special word, that's why we reserve it for certain special people. Not every fireman and policeman who was on duty that day was a hero. The ones who risked or lost their lives trying to rescue people were heroes. They acted heroically. The others probably did a good job and were very helpful, but heroes?

If everyone's a hero, then the word doesn't mean much anymore. And sooner or later we'll have to give the real heroes (the heroic ones) a new name, to distinguish them from the rest of the pack. Too bad "superheroes" is already taken; it would have been perfect. But relax, folks, if I know us, "megahero" can't be too far over the horizon. Although to be honest, I kind of like the alliteration in "hyperhero." Let's shoot for that.

PLEASE DON'T SAY THAT

Here is a small sampling of embarrassing societal clichés that I find tiresome and, in some cases, just plain ignorant.

If It Saves Just One Life

You often hear a new policy or procedure justified by the specious idea that "If it saves the life of just one (insert here 'child' or 'American soldier'), it will be worth it." Well, maybe not. Maybe a closer look would show that the cost in time, money, or inconvenience would be much too high to justify merely saving one life. What's wrong with looking at it like that? Governments and corporations make those calculations all the time.

Every Child Is Special

An empty and meaningless sentiment. What about every adult? Isn't every adult special? And if not, then at what age does a person go from being special to being not-so-special? And if every adult *is* also special, then that means all people are special and the idea has no meaning. This embarrassing sentiment is usually advanced to further some position that is either political or fund-raising in nature. It's similar to "children are our future." It's completely meaningless and is probably being used in some self-serving way.

He's Smiling Down

After the death of some person (even many years after) you will often hear someone refer to the deceased by saying, "I get the feeling he's up there now, smiling down on us. And I think he's pleased." I actually heard this when some dead coach's son was being inducted into the Football Hall of Fame.

First of all, it's extremely doubtful that there's any "up there" to smile down from. It's poetic, and I guess it's comforting. But it probably doesn't exist. Besides, if a person *did* somehow survive death in a non-physical form, he would be far too busy with other things to be smiling down on people.

And why is it we never hear that someone is "smiling up at us." I suppose it doesn't occur to people that a loved one might be in hell. And in that case the person in question probably wouldn't be smiling. More likely, he'd be screaming. "I get the feeling he's down there now, screaming up at us. And I think he's in pain." People just refuse to be realistic.

This Puts Everything in Perspective

This nonsense will often crop up after some unexpected sports death like that of Cardinals pitcher Darryl Kile. After one of these athletes' sudden death, one of his dopey teammates will say, "This really puts everything in perspective." And I say, listen, putz, if you need someone to die in order to put things in perspective, you've got problems. You ain't payin' enough attention.

America's Lost Innocence

I keep hearing that America lost its innocence on 9/11. I thought that happened when JFK was shot. Or was it Vietnam? Pearl Harbor? How many times can America lose its innocence? Maybe we keep finding it again. Doubtful. Because, actually, if you look at the record, you'll find that America has had very little innocence from the beginning.

Let the Healing Begin

This bothersome sentiment is usually heard following some large-scale killing or accident that's been overreported in the news. Like Columbine, Oklahoma City, or the World Trade Center. It's often accompanied by another meaningless, over-worked cliché, "closure." People can't seem to get it through their heads that there is never any healing or closure. Ever. There is only a short pause before the next "horrifying" event. People forget there is such a thing as memory, and that when a wound "heals" it leaves a permanent scar that never goes away, but merely fades a little. What really ought to be said after one of these so-called tragedies is, "Let the scarring begin." Just trying to be helpful here.

THE FANATICS WILL WIN

I hope you good, loyal Americans understand that in the long run the Islamist extremists are going to win. Because you can't beat numbers, and you can't beat fanaticism—the willingness to die for an idea.

A country like ours, preoccupied with Jet Skis, off-road vehicles, snow boards, Jacuzzis, microwave ovens, pornography, lap dances, massage parlors, escort services, panty liners, penis enhancement, tummy tucks, thongs, and Odor Eaters doesn't have a prayer—not even a good, old-fashioned Christian prayer—against a billion fanatics who hate that country, detest its materialism, and have nothing really to lose. Maybe fifty years ago, but not today when germs and chemicals and nuclear materials are for sale everywhere.

People who don't give a shit and have nothing to lose will always prevail over people who are fighting for some vague sentiment scrawled on a piece of parchment. Folks, they're gonna getcha; and it ain't gonna be pleasant.

We can't drop a five-thousand-pound bomb on every one of them. They will either run all over us or, in trying, they will turn us into even bigger monsters than we already are.

And don't get all excited about this goofy idea, "the spread of democracy." No matter who the United States puts in charge to bring peace and order in Iraq or Palestine or anywhere else, those people will be killed. It's that simple. Anyone who supports the United States will be killed. Peace and order will not be tolerated. Start saving your cash for the black market, folks, you're gonna need it.

CELEBRITY CRYSTAL BALL

I predict Charles Manson will be released from prison and record another album. This time people will listen.

Hollywood movie stars will continue to adopt Third World children and those children will continue to grow up socially maladjusted.

I predict former president Bill Clinton will be found in bed with a transsexual and claim on national television, "I did not have sex with those people."

I predict that, while taping an AIDS special in Africa, Geraldo Rivera will catch the syph from a native.

Jimmy Hoffa will be found alive, living with a family of gibbons.

Elvis Presley will be seen sneaking into a Swiss Porta-Potty with a suitcase full of cheese burritos.

I predict that, as a practical joke, Henry Kissinger will have his bladder removed and overnighted to Renée Zellweger.

I predict Liza Minnelli will decide never to get married again, although she will continue to get divorced.

During a party at Larry Flynt's house, Gary Coleman will disappear forever inside the vagina of Anna Nicole Smith.

I predict Defense Secretary Donald Rumsfeld will be found unconscious in an Iraqi police barracks with goat semen in his hair.

Britain's playful Prince William will play a royal prank on several members of the Irish press—and get the royal shit beat out of him.

Charles Gibson and Diane Sawyer will resign from ABC News and hitchhike across Canada wearing his and her pirate costumes.

Heidi Fleiss will reveal that during a one-night stand with Don Ho, following each orgasm, they ran around the room screaming, "Heidi Ho!"

Condoleezza Rice will attend a European ministers' conference with five pounds of potato salad stuffed in her brassiere.

The long string of Kennedy-family tragedies will come to an end at a reunion in Massachusetts when all remaining members are wiped out in a hotel fire.

Prince Charles and Camilla Parker Bowles will name their firstborn Eileen the Cocksucker. Other members of the Royal Family will fail to see the humor.

I predict Shirley MacLaine will reveal that in various past lives she has been an explorer, an empress, a priestess, and a Maxi-pad.

I predict Al Roker will sleepwalk into a Dunkin' Donuts and eat six dozen lemon custards. All the staples in his stomach will pop at once and six policemen will be killed.

I predict Bing Crosby will return from the dead and beat the shit out of Joan Crawford's grandchildren.

The Vatican will reveal that in 1996, when John Paul II's plane landed near the South Pole, in keeping with his custom he kissed the tarmac, and his lips stuck to the ground.

While seated on the *Tonight Show* panel, Rudolph Giuliani will fall asleep and have a vigorous wet dream. Jay will go to commercial.

A new biography of Jacqueline Onassis will reveal that as a young woman she fell in love with a poor man, but immediately ended the affair when she realized her mistake.

I predict Chuck Woolery will host a new game show based on guessing the size of a woman's bush.

Sharon Osbourne will claim she can accurately predict stock market trends by analyzing the stains in Ozzy's shorts.

Gary Busey will suffer multiple spine injuries while engaging in rough sex with a family of Montana brown bears.

I predict Rio de Janeiro will rename its main thoroughfare after the Mills Brothers.

I predict that the popular host of *Jeopardy!*, Alex Trebek, will be killed by the Mob because he knows too much.

Hollywood will revive a popular series of 1940s jungle movies when Russell Crowe stars in *Tarzan Fucks a Zebra*.

Connie Chung will reveal that the late Sonny Bono speaks to her in dreams and is relaying accurate tips on Powerball numbers.

I predict that, as a publicity stunt for a new line of human growth hormones, Paul Simon, Tom Cruise, and Paul Anka will be laid end to end and measure just under twelve feet.

The scandals in the Catholic Church will continue as a group of seminarians in Italy are found to be manually pleasuring zoo animals.

Pat Robertson, Jerry Falwell, and Billy Graham will lead a nationwide prayer vigil and ask God to do something about America's moral climate. God will promptly strike all three of them dead.

And finally: Watch for Dom DeLuise to explode fairly soon.

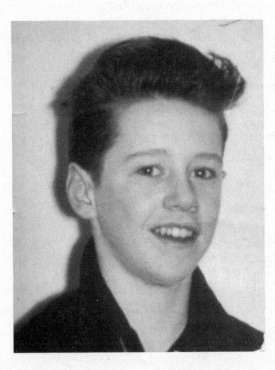

EUPHEMISMS:
DEATH AND DYING

Some of our best work with euphemisms involves the subject that makes us the most uncomfortable: death.

Our most common euphemism for death is to say the person *passed away*. Or *passed on*. If you believe in an afterlife, you may prefer *crossed over*; or *crossed over to the other side*. Whenever I hear that someone has crossed over to the other side, I always picture Fifth Avenue.

Then there's the official term for dying, the doctor term. In this case the person simply *expires*. Like a magazine subscription. One month he just doesn't show up. Unfortunately, he can't renew. Or so they say. Better check with the Hindus on that.

Now, continuing. In this current age of specialization—and increasing detachment—if the person in question dies in a hospital, it's called a *terminal episode*. Although the insurance company sees it as *negative patient-care outcome*. That one's actually kinda nice, isn't it? And if the negative patient-care outcome was caused by medical malpractice, then it's referred to it as a *therapeutic misadventure*. Colorful term. No wonder so many doctors are leaving their practices; it's hard to get therapeutic-misadventure insurance.

But by far the most creative terms we've come up with to comfort ourselves about death are the ones that describe the rituals survivors put themselves through. We owe a lot of this softened language to the funeral business. Or, as they prefer to be known, the *death-care industry*. They have completely transformed the language used to describe what happens following a death.

In years past it went like this: "The *old man died*, so the *undertaker* picked up the *body*, brought it to the *funeral home* and put it in a *casket*. People sent *flowers* and held a *wake*. After the *funeral*, they put the *coffin* in a *hearse* and drove it to the *cemetery*, where the *dead man* was *buried* in a *grave*."

But in these days of heightened sensitivity, the same series of events produces what sounds like a completely different experience: "The *senior citizen passed away*, so the *funeral director* claimed the *remains* of the *decedent*, took them to the *memorial chapel*, and placed them in a *burial container*. *Grieving survivors* sent *floral tributes* to be displayed in the *slumber room*, where the *grief coordinator* conducted the *viewing*. Following the *memorial service*, the *funeral coach* transported the *departed* to the *garden of remembrance* where his *human remains* were *interred* in their *final resting place*."

Huh? What's that? Did someone die or something?

IT'S NO BULLSHIT!

AN ASTOUNDING COLLECTION OF AMAZING STORIES FROM THE SECRET FILES OF *BELIEVE IT OR ELSE* MAGAZINE. READ THESE ASTONISHING FACTS AND FEEL YOUR FUCKIN' BRAIN MELT.

The sun does not really give off light. It merely appears to give off light because everything around it is so dark.

The Belzini tribe of South American Indians will eventually be extinct, because they initiate their young by putting them to death at the age of three.

During her entire sixty-four-year reign, Queen Victoria never once went to the bathroom. She said she was holding it in for a more appropriate time. Her words were, "We don't have to go just now."

Indianapolis, the capital of Indiana, is actually located in Brazil. It only seems to be in Indiana when viewed on a map.

When the Alexander Farkington family moved from Boston to San Diego, they had to leave their dog, Peckerhead, behind. Miraculously, two weeks later the dog showed up in Key West, Florida. Mistakenly, Peckerhead had taken Interstate 95 south instead of getting on the Massachusetts Turnpike.

Contrary to popular belief, Babe Ruth did not call his famous home-run shot. He was actually giving the finger to a hot-dog vendor who had cheated him out of twelve cents.

Incredibly, there was no Hitler. There is no record of any such person. It's true, there was a little German man with a small moustache who combed his hair to one side and started World War II. He also killed six million Jews. But he was not Hitler. He was, in fact, a shoemaker named Hank Fleck.

A cheetah is actually slower than an armadillo. It only appears to be faster, because the armadillo moves so slowly.

Unbelievably, a goldfish can kill a gorilla. However, it does require a substantial element of surprise.

It's now possible to travel completely around the world without money or credit cards. You must be prepared, however, to walk and swim extremely long distances.

A forty-two-year-old man from Ballbender, Wyoming, drove a riding lawn mower backward from Vermont to Argentina. The trip put him under such stress that he is now incapable of thought.

The pyramids are not really old. They were built in 1943 as a joke by drunken Italian soldiers on leave in Egypt at the time. All photographs of the area taken before that time have been retouched.

The sky is not blue. It merely looks that way because blue is the name we have given that color.

Two times two is not four. It is nine. Actually, everything is nine except seventeen. Seventeen is actually six.

Placing a two-hundred-pound pile of cooked garlic, dogshit, and chocolate chips on the doorstep of your newly purchased home will keep your enemies away. However, it will not prevent your new neighbors from considering you a family that bears watching.

The record for the greatest amount of Jell-O in one location belongs to Lemon Lime, Minnesota, where residents poured twenty thousand boxes of Jell-O into a lake and heated it, just to claim the title. Most of them are happy with the results. However, some local residents, diving in the shallow areas, claim to have hit their heads on small pieces of fruit cocktail.

BELIEVE IT OR ELSE, BUT IT'S NO BULLSHIT!

RULES TO LIVE BY

Life is not as difficult as people think; all one needs is a good set of rules. Since it is probably too late for you, here are some guidelines to pass along to your children.

1. Relax and take it easy. Don't get caught up in hollow conceits such as "doing something with your life." Such twaddle is outmoded and a sure formula for disappointment.

2. Whatever it is you pursue, try to do it just well enough to remain in the middle third of the field. Keep your thoughts and ideas to yourself and don't ask questions. Remember, the squeaky wheel is the first one to be replaced.

3. Size people up quickly, and develop rigid attitudes based on your first impression. If you try to delve deeper and get to "know" people, you're asking for trouble.

4. Don't fall for that superstitious nonsense about treating people the way you would like to be treated. It is a transparently narcissistic approach, and may be the sign of a weak mind.

5. Spend as much time as you can pleasing and impressing others, even if it makes you unhappy. Pay special attention to shallow manipulators who can do you the most harm. Remember, in the overall scheme, you count for very little.

6. Surround yourself with inferiors and losers. Not only will you look good by comparison, but they will look up to you, and that will make you feel better.

7. Don't buy into the sentimental notion that everyone has shortcomings; it's the surest way of undermining yourself. Remember, the really best people have no defects. If you're not perfect, something is wrong.

8. If by some off chance you do detect a few faults, first, accept the fact that you are probably deeply flawed. Then make a list of your faults and dwell on them. Carry the list around and try to think of things to add. Blame yourself for everything.

9. Beware of intuition and gut instincts, they are completely unreliable. Instead, develop preconceived notions and don't waver unless someone tells you to. Then change your mind and adopt their point of view. But only if they seem to know what they're talking about.

10. Never give up on an idea simply because it is bad and doesn't work. Cling to it even when it is hopeless. Anyone can cut and run, but it takes a very special person to stay with something that is stupid and harmful.

11. Always remember, today doesn't count. Trying to make something out of today only robs you of precious time that could be spent daydreaming or resting up.

12. Try to dwell on the past. Think of all the mistakes you've made, and how much better it would be if you hadn't made them. Think of what you should have done, and blame yourself for not doing so. And don't go easy. Be really hard on yourself.

13. If by chance you make a fresh mistake, especially a costly one, try to repeat it a few times so you become familiar with it and can do it easily in the future. Write it down. Put it with your list of faults.

14. Beware also of the dangerous trap of looking ahead; it will only get you in trouble. Instead, try to drift along from day to day in a meandering fashion. Don't get sidetracked with some foolish "plan."

15. Finally, enjoy yourself all the time, and do whatever you want. Don't be seduced by that mindless chatter going around about "responsibility." That's exactly the sort of thing that can ruin your life.

A MODERN MAN

I'm a modern man,
digital and smoke-free;
a man for the millennium.

A diversified, multi-cultural,
post-modern deconstructionist;
politically, anatomically, and ecologically incorrect.

I've been uplinked and downloaded,
I've been inputted and outsourced.
I know the upside of downsizing,
I know the downside of upgrading.

I'm a high-tech low-life.
A cutting-edge, state-of-the-art,
bi-coastal multi-tasker,
and I can give you a gigabyte in a nanosecond.

I'm new-wave, but I'm old-school;
and my inner child is outward-bound.

I'm a hot-wired, heat-seeking,
warm-hearted cool customer;
voice-activated and bio-degradable.

I interface with my database;
my database is in cyberspace;
so I'm interactive, I'm hyperactive,
and from time to time I'm radioactive.

Behind the eight ball, ahead of the curve,
ridin' the wave, dodgin' the bullet,
pushin' the envelope.

I'm on point, on task, on message,
and off drugs.

I've got no need for coke and speed;
I've got no urge to binge and purge.

I'm in the moment, on the edge,
over the top, but under the radar.

A high-concept, low-profile,
medium-range ballistic missionary.

A street-wise smart bomb.
A top-gun bottom-feeder.

I wear power ties, I tell power lies,
I take power naps, I run victory laps.

*I'm a totally ongoing, big-foot, slam-dunk
rainmaker with a pro-active outreach.*

*A raging workaholic, a working rageaholic;
out of rehab and in denial.*

*I've got a personal trainer,
a personal shopper,
a personal assistant,
and a personal agenda.*

*You can't shut me up;
you can't dumb me down.*

*'Cause I'm tireless, and I'm wireless.
I'm an alpha-male on beta-blockers.*

*I'm a non-believer,
I'm an over-achiever;
Laid-back and fashion-forward.
Up-front, down-home;
low-rent, high-maintenance.*

*I'm super-sized, long-lasting,
high-definition, fast-acting,
oven-ready, and built to last.*

*A hands-on, footloose, knee-jerk head case;
prematurely post-traumatic,
and I have a love child who sends me hate-mail.*

But I'm feeling, I'm caring,
I'm healing, I'm sharing.
A supportive, bonding, nurturing
primary-care giver.

My output is down, but my income is up.
I take a short position on the long bond,
and my revenue stream has its own cash flow.

I read junk mail, I eat junk food,
I buy junk bonds, I watch trash sports.

I'm gender-specific, capital-intensive,
user-friendly, and lactose-intolerant.

I like rough sex; I like tough love.
I use the f-word in my e-mail.
And the software on my hard drive
is hard-core—no soft porn.

I bought a microwave at a mini-mall.
I bought a mini-van at a mega-store.
I eat fast food in the slow lane.

I'm toll-free, bite-size, ready-to-wear,
and I come in all sizes.

A fully equipped, factory-authorized,
hospital-tested, clinically proven,
scientifically formulated medical miracle.

I've been pre-washed, pre-cooked, pre-heated,
pre-screened, pre-approved, pre-packaged,
post-dated, freeze-dried, double-wrapped,
and vacuum-packed.

And . . . I have unlimited broadband capacity.

I'm a rude dude, but I'm the real deal.
Lean and mean.
Cocked, locked, and ready to rock;
rough, tough, and hard to bluff.

I take it slow, I go with the flow;
I ride with the tide, I've got glide in my stride.

Drivin' and movin', sailin' and spinnin';
jivin' and groovin', wailin' and winnin'.

I don't snooze, so I don't lose.
I keep the pedal to the metal
and the rubber on the road.
I party hearty, and lunchtime is crunch time.

I'm hangin' in, there ain't no doubt;
and I'm hangin' tough.
Over and out.